C000256035

ALEX QUICK is the pseudonym of an English novelist. He is the author of *102 Free Things to Do, 102 Ways to Write a Novel, 102 Ways to Improve your Partner, 102 English Things to Do, 102 Things to Do in Summer* and *102 Things to Do in Autumn*. There will be more...

102
THINGS TO DO
IN WINTER

Also by Alex Quick

102 Free Things to Do
102 Ways to Write a Novel
102 English Things to Do
102 Ways to Improve your Partner
102 Things to Do in Autumn
102 Things to Do in Spring
102 Things to Do in Summer

First published in 2013 by Old Street Publishing Ltd,
Trebinshun House, Brecon LD3 7PX
www.oldstreetpublishing.co.uk

ISBN 978 1 908699 38 1

Copyright © Alex Quick, 2013

The right of Alex Quick to be identified as the author of this work has been asserted by him in accordance with the Copyright, Designs and Patents Act 1988.

All rights reserved. No part of this publication may be reproduced, stored in or introduced into a retrieval system, or transmitted, in any form, or by any means (electronic, mechanical, photocopying, recording or otherwise) without the prior written permission of the publisher.

10 9 8 7 6 5 4 3 2 1

A CIP catalogue record for this title is available from the British Library.
Printed and bound in Great Britain

To Dad

102
THINGS TO DO
IN WINTER

ALEX QUICK

CONTENTS

1.

STAY AT AN ICE HOTEL

You might think you could stay at an ice hotel at any old time of the year. In fact, ice hotels are only created and run in winter. Artificial refrigeration is too expensive to keep on in summer, and ice hotels rely on the winter weather to stop the establishment melting and drowning the guests.

In an ice hotel you stay in rooms made of ice with doors, walls, ceilings and furniture of ice, on a bed of ice. Although the bed is a hard block of frozen water, your night's sleep is made possible with the use of furs and sleeping bags. For your convenience there may be a trouser-press made of ice. There are no hot showers, however.

Downstairs in the ice bar, surrounded by ice sculptures, you sip icy drinks from glasses made of ice (a drink 'in the rocks' rather than 'on the rocks') and exchange icy small-talk and icy glances.

Ice hotels are found in many parts of the world, such as the USA, Canada, Scandinavia and Japan, but the first ice hotel was in Sweden, in the village of Jukkasjärvi: it opened in 1990 and is seasonally reconstructed every year with a different design. Alongside the hotel (with rooms for 100 guests) is an ice church with ice pews and an altar of ice, in which worshippers are exhorted to open their freezing hearts.

2.

GO SLEDDING

This is the most democratic of the winter sports. Babies on tea-trays; geriatrics on plastic bags. Anything that will slide down snow. In fact, the more basic types of conveyance are sometimes faster. A piece of plastic sheeting held up at the front can outpace an old-fashioned sled with steel runners.

Sledding is not an exact science (though it's more exact than snow tubing – see §52), and steering may be a problem. A good way to steer is to use the feet. Bearing down on the snow on one side creates drag and inclines the sled to that side, so if you want to go left, put your foot down left, and if right, right. (However, if despite your efforts you look like you're going to crash into a telephone pole, fence, tree or polar cow, I'd advise you to bail out and take whatever contusions are coming to you rather than endure a head-on impact.)

To increase speed at the start, take a run-up at your sled and throw yourself onto it. Actually this is a good way to start a sled race. Take up positions a short distance behind your sleds and then, on a signal, run towards your vehicles. If you don't do this, sled races tend to begin in a rather lustreless manner, with everyone waiting for gravity to start working.

One type of sledding that you may not care to try is Hawaiian lava sledding (or he'ehōlua). This involves riding a twenty-foot war sled down a lava field at speeds of up to 70 miles per hour (110 km/h), emitting savage cries to honour Pele, the goddess of fire.

3.

GO TO AN ICE SCULPTURE FESTIVAL

Ice sculpture is the closest the decorative arts get to the condition of music: no sooner do you experience it than it melts away. Ice is a material both solid and ethereal, which is the key to its fascination.

Modern ice sculpture began with a legendary Parisian, the chef Auguste Escoffier, who made swans from ice to amaze his dinner guests. Since then, ice swans have become rather passé. Ice sculptures can be anything, from human figures to swarms of bees, or even entire buildings that can be walked on and in. Occasionally sculptures are made from different colours of ice (created using dyes), sometimes with lights frozen inside so they are illuminated from within.

There are festivals, ice-carving competitions and ice

sculpture trails in many major cities throughout the world. One of the biggest festivals is the International Ice and Snow Sculpture Festival at Harbin in China, where an entire city is created every year from ice and snow and lit up by lasers. Harbin freezes solid every winter, so there is no shortage of raw materials.

At some festivals there are workshops where you can try your hand yourself, although since most large sculptures are roughed out with chainsaws, you'll need to serve an apprenticeship.

4.

GO TO MIDNIGHT MASS

It's a shame that most people no longer go to church at Christmas. Even in a post-Christian society, Christmas is still a Christian feast, and without some understanding of the Christmas story, Christmas is just a depressing means of gaining extra fat.

Standing for a couple of hours in a church, if nothing else, gives you the space to reflect on the passing year. In the immortal and non-denominational words of John Lennon: 'So this is Christmas… and what have you done?'

Or think of it this way: a typical congregation, not just on Christmas Eve but on any normal Sunday, is as much a communion of doubt as a communion of faith. Those who attend church fit somewhere in the spectrum from fervent conviction to dyed-in the-wool scepticism. If you attend church with no beliefs, it doesn't mean you don't belong: it merely means that you represent the atheist end of the spectrum.

What's so stirring about midnight mass is that is mixes the sacred and the profane. Easter is arguably a more significant festival, because it represents the moment (Christians believe) that Christ redeemed mankind, but Easter is perhaps only fully accessible by the faithful. Christmas Eve, in contrast, is about something everyone can relate to: the moment when a baby was born in poverty and loved by ordinary people, and about the sanctity, innocence and beauty of a new human life.

5.

COMMEMORATE THE EGGNOG RIOT

The Eggnog Riot took place at the US military academy of West Point in 1826. Angered at a decree that their Christmas was to be alcohol-free, the cadets smuggled cases of whiskey into the academy, made eggnog with it, and then, according to a contemporary account, 'reeled through the barracks shouting, some with swords, some with muskets, some with bayonets; one fired a musket; another threw a log at an officer.'

How strange that they chose eggnog. To most of us it is associated with sleepy post-prandial uncles. There is something tranquil about it, combining as it does the comforting and maternal ingredients of eggs and milk. You can even make it without alcohol, practically as a drink of the nursery.

But let's say you want to make some with a hint of Christmas tonic.

To serve four people, take two eggs and separate them into yolks and whites. Beat the whites until they are foamy, then mix them back with the yolks. Now take half a cup of whipping cream and beat that until it is stiff. Fold two tablespoons of caster sugar (don't use ordinary granulated sugar or the mixture will be grainy) into the cream. Stir in the eggs, then a cup of milk and half a cup of the alcohol. Eggnog should be thick and creamy, so make sure you fold all the ingredients together by hand: an electric mixer will dispel all the air bubbles.

And that's it: eggnog, or as they say in France, 'Lait de Poule'.

If you're allergic to milk, try a 'Soy nog' or even a 'Tofu nog' (with creamed tofu instead of dairy cream).

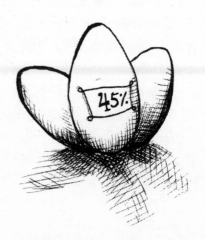

6.

MAKE MULLED WINE

Another seasonal grog-cup is mulled wine. You can buy this ready-prepared in bottles, but it is always bland and unexciting, an 'all things to all men' sort of drink, and not really in tune with the spirit of the season. Home-made mulled wine is much tastier and more aromatic.

First, get a couple of bottles of red wine – not too cheap, because even covered up with tons of cloves, a really cheap red wine can be quite disgusting – pour them in a large pan and add three oranges cut into segments. Do the same with a lemon and a lime, leaving a couple of thin slices for garnish. Add about eight cloves, plus a cinnamon stick, some grated nutmeg and about six tablespoons of sugar. Other flavours such as ginger and bay leaves work well. Now heat the mixture up. But don't allow it to boil! Boiling will evaporate off the alcohol, and instead of intoxicating wine you'll have intoxicating wallpaper. Heat only to a gentle simmer for about ten minutes. Then take the mixture off and allow it to steep. Steeping lets the hot wine, spices and citrus flavours interpenetrate.

When party time comes, give the liquid another warm-up and serve immediately. If serving in glasses, you can create a garnish from the remaining orange, lemon or lime slices, studded with cloves and perched on the rim. If ladling from the bowl, include a slice or two of fruit in the glass.

7.

MAKE A SPICED APPLE CHRISTMAS CAKE

Christmas cake comes in a variety of types. In fact, any cake you wish to call a Christmas cake is a Christmas cake, even a sponge cake with strawberries on top (that's what they call a Christmas cake in Japan).

Most Christmas cakes, though, it's fair to say, are rich in fruit and very dark and heavy. Spiced apple cake, on the other hand, is lighter and more digestible, and can be served with custard, cream, ice cream or eggnog custard at the end of a hefty Christmas dinner.

To make the cake you need to combine the following ingredients (it doesn't matter much in what order as long as the eggs don't curdle): a cup of muscovado sugar, four eggs, a cup of butter, two cups of plain flour, a cup and a half of peeled, finely-chopped apple, a teaspoon of baking powder, a half cup of softened raisins, a tablespoon of honey, a tablespoon of milk, a teaspoon of vanilla extract, and spices to taste (about half a teaspoon each of cinnamon, nutmeg and ground cloves makes a nice combination). Pour the mixture into a ring-shaped tin if you have one, or into a large baking tin. Bake at 350 degrees (gas mark 4) for 30 minutes.

This is a treat that needs no special ingredients and can be whipped up in an hour, but is perfect for Christmas. Dust with icing sugar and serve with a sprig of holly on top if desired.

8.

GO WOK RACING

This is similar to bobsledding, except you put your bottom in a wok. The hands and feet dangle outside, though they may be protected by being fitted with ladles (you see the culinary connection).

For those suspecting I have made this up for the purpose of filling the pages of this book, it is a real sport, though it has not yet been given the imprimatur of a Winter Olympic event. It started in Germany in the early 2000s as a stunt for the German TV show *Wetten, dass..?* (Rough translation: 'You wanna bet?') The show co-opted various hard-bottomed German TV personalities to race each other in woks on a bobsled track. The idea caught on, and wok-racing championships began to be held annually, though they were always won by the same man, George Hackl, who happens to be an Olympic luge champion. (A British version of this phenomenon occurred when

Stirling Moss persisted in winning the all the trophies in lawnmower racing.) Hackl is also known as the 'Speeding Weisswurst', because he looks like a white sausage in his shining silver bodysuit.

Team events are also held, utilizing four woks welded together onto a frame.

The woks themselves are ordinary kitchen woks, slightly modified for safety: the edge of a wok can be rather sharp, and therefore not necessarily a good thing to have close to your posterior when travelling at high speed. Accordingly they are fitted with rubber rims.

9.

PLAY SNOW SNAKE

Snow Snake is a traditional game of various Native American nations, among them the Iroquois and Sioux. It involves throwing a length of wood down a specially-prepared track in the snow. The length of wood that goes furthest is the winner. Snow snake has a particular cultural significance for native Americans. It's a 'medicine' that promotes social good and initiates young boys into the tribe.

The creation of the track is the complicated bit. It's made by piling up snow into a long bank, a couple of feet high but hundreds of yards long: the finished product looks like an embankment for a model railway. Running down the centre is a groove or trough, about 5 inches (12 cm) deep and the same wide. This is the channel down which the 'snakes' run, a sort of bobsled track for sticks.

The type of stick used is part of the art: sticks can

be various lengths, from little ones a few inches long to poles as long as a spear. The poles are covered in varnish to make them glide faster and further, and are fitted with a lead tip: often the sticks are handed down from father to son. Teams take it in turns to throw their sticks down the channel. Stories of sticks travelling hundreds of yards are common.

10.

BECOME A POLAR BEAR
OR A WALRUS

… by going swimming in winter. In the USA, winter swimmers are known as 'polar bears', and 'polar bear clubs', which meet to take a dip on New Year's Day or Christmas Day, are popular in many states. In Russia the same people are called 'walruses'.

The activity is not limited to these two countries. Winter swimming has a global fan base, particularly in very cold countries such as Finland, Sweden and the United Kingdom. Why people don't swim in freezing water in Rome or Seville isn't immediately clear, but perhaps they just have more sense.

In London the best-known winter swimming is to be had at Highgate Ponds in Hampstead and at the Serpentine in Hyde Park. The latter hosts the annual Peter Pan Christmas Day race, inaugurated in 1904 by JM Barrie, the creator of the eponymous never-growing-up boy.

Swimming in really freezing conditions (where ice is beginning to form) can be dangerous and should only be attempted by people who swim regularly in very cold open water. Hypothermia is a real possibility. Having said that, many 'ice-swimmers' swear by its health benefits.

It also provides an excellent excuse to built up a layer of subcutaneous fat.

11.

DROP YOUR TROUSERS

In winter? Definitely. The No Pants Subway Ride started in New York in January 2002 and has now spread to other cities worldwide.

It was tastefully minimalistic at first, the equivalent of a pair of Marks and Spencer's plain navy Y-fronts. Only seven people took part, removing their outer lower garments as the train rattled between stations. The following year several dozen others joined in. Then the idea was picked up in Mexico City, Rome, London, Stockholm and Shanghai. All hell broke loose. The equivalent in underwear terms? A ruffed thong featuring an appliqué head of Che Guevara. Social media exacerbated the phenomenon, giving a new dimension to the term 'flash mob'. Thousands of people started taking part, the trouserless straphangers outnumbering the trousered. Arrests began. Fortunately the no-pants activists – though no spokesman could be found to explain exactly what they were protesting against – found a sympathetic judge who ruled that it was 'not illegal to wear underwear in public'.

And so it continues. Winter is sometimes the least respectable of the seasons.

12.

GO SNOWSHOEING

Snowshoeing is a fast-growing winter sport that anyone of any age can participate in. It's cheap and it's simple: it just involves strapping snowshoes to your feet and getting out there in beautiful snow-covered scenery, perhaps for walking, but also for running, climbing or accessing back-country ski or snowboard trails.

Snowshoes, because they are large and flat, work by distributing weight over a wide area. You don't sink but float. The ancient inventors of snowshoes probably got the idea from observing Snowshoe hares, which have extended hairy feet for skittering over snowdrifts.

As well as snowshoes, you need poles: these are important to help you maintain balance, but also enable you to brake when going downhill.

Snowshoeing makes difficult mountain terrain easily accessible. Many resorts have established snowshoe trails, but further safety can be assured by taking GPS tracking equipment, plus maps, a compass, a phone and an avalanche beacon (a device that sends out a distress call). And sandwiches.

Start on flatter terrain before you get ambitious, but after a while you'll be able to climb hillsides. The design incorporates a free heel, rather like in Telemark or cross-country skiing, making snowshoes very manoeuvrable. So manoeuvrable in fact that snowshoe hurdling is a recognised event in the Arctic Winter Games.

13.

READ WAR AND PEACE

Why in winter? Well, think about it: Napoleon invading Russia...the Battle of Borodino... the sack of Moscow... the French retreat in the winter of 1812 in which the Grande Armée lost more than three-quarters of its men to starvation and frostbite... all very nice to read about if you are sitting in front of a fire with a cup of hot chocolate (see §28). The cynical and ambitious Prince Bolkonsky, the spirited, suffering Natasha Rostov, the self-doubting Pierre Bezukhov, the long chapters of philosophical pondering, make this one of the greatest, most indispensable – and most unclassifiable – works of world literature. It's a sort of Moby-Dick on land, and a perfect treat for the winter, when a million words suddenly doesn't seem so long.

After *War and Peace* why not tackle some more winter-themed Russian books? Gogol's St Petersburg tales might be a good start ('The Overcoat', 'The Nose'), set in the freezing northern capital of Russia. Or try Solzhenitsyn's *One Day in the Life of Ivan Denisovitch*: that should have you longing for a food parcel. Or Chekhov's diary of his journey to a Russian penal colony, *The Island of Sakhalin*, where he witnessed 'the extreme limits of man's degradation' amid bitter winter conditions. Or Dostoevsky's *The House of the Dead*, set in a Siberian gulag.

When it comes to writing about winter, the Russians do it better than anyone else.

14.

GO ON A GHOST WALK

On winter nights, fear breeds. The dark descends quickly. The trees poke up their iron fingers, and in their wet trunks we see eyes, skulls. Bats flutter and squeak. The wind howls like an abandoned child. In the air is the smell of rotting things.

Winter, in short, is an ideal time to go on a ghost walk.

Fortunately these are hugely popular, and there's bound to be one near you. There are ghost walks in Edinburgh, Nottingham, Norwich, Chester, York and London (though none in Stevenage); further afield there are ghost walks in Paris (*Les Mystères de Paris*) and Madrid (*Tour de fantasmas de Madrid*). The older towns, those that have had time to accumulate catalogues of the most gruesome infamy, are the best. Debased monks who murdered penitents and then sold their bones as relics! The very spot where a woman and her thirteen-year-old son were hanged, drawn and quartered! Can you still feel the hangman's breath on your neck?

Or perhaps you would care (or dare) to visit Pluckley in Kent, the most haunted village in England. Perhaps you are bold enough (or foolish enough) to spend a night (or an hour) in the Screaming Woods. Or wait for the haunted coach and four to appear on Maltman's Hill. Or see the place by the abandoned railway line where the Watercress Woman was burned to death.

A sudden chill has descended on this book. It may be best to move on.

15.

GO TO A PANTO

Pantomime comes from the Greek *pantos*, meaning 'all', and *mimos*, meaning 'imitation'. Pantomimes in the ancient world were rather closer to what we might call variety shows, with music, dancing and risqué humour. They were roundly denounced by serious writers of the classical theatre, who deplored the lack of characters being blinded or tricked into marrying their mothers, and were probably jealous of the box-office.

The all-singing, all-dancing style of early pantomimes has survived in the English pantomime theatre (pantomime is performed in other parts of the world but not with the same level of devotion), but the actual stories are now based on traditional children's tales such as Cinderella, Jack and the Beanstalk or Puss in Boots. Pantos are a traditional winter entertainment, and do an essential job in propping up playhouses for the rest of the year. Along with the nativity play (see §44) they represent most children's first experience of theatre.

If you go to a pantomime, expect to join in. You will be required to sing, cheer, boo and call out 'He's behind you!', and may be hauled onto the stage to take part in a love-duet with the Dame, possibly a celebrity from ITV. Research has shown that the best place to sit if you don't want to be forced to perform is the Upper Circle, Row E, Seat 15, but Widow Twankey may have read this research and seek you out in precisely this spot.

16.

VISIT A GERMAN MARKET

What is a German market? Well, it's a rather beautiful blend of the commercial and the religious. The stalls at a German market sell Teutonic foodstuffs such as *Lebkuchen* and *Glühwein*, but there are also performances of traditional plays and dances, plus carol-singing and nativity scenes. You have to go to Germany to experience a really good German market – to Dresden's 'Striezelmarkt', named after a type of Christmas cake, or Nuremberg's 'Christkindlesmarkt', named after the 'Christkind' or Christ child – but there are imitation German markets in cities around the world: Birmingham and New York have their own German markets, for example.

The Christ child is actually a rather interesting figure. A German version of Father Christmas, only younger and without a beard, he was popularised by Martin Luther in the 16th century as a replacement for St Nick. The Christ child visits German children on Christmas Eve and brings presents. When the presents have been laid at the foot of the tree, his departure is announced by the ringing of a small silver bell (done secretly by the parents, some say). Various German cities elect a real child every year to play the role of the Christ child at the Christmas market, with different cities adopting different traditions. In Nuremberg, the Christ child is always an attractive young woman between the ages of 16 and 19. Among her qualifications she must be 'at least 1.6 meters tall, and vertigo- and weather-proof'.

17

PREPARE A TURDUCKEN

Nothing says the holiday season like three animals stuffed into one another. This is a process known as engastration, and the best known engastration recipe is turducken, in which a de-boned turkey is stuffed with a de-boned duck, which is then stuffed with a de-boned chicken. (The bones of the ribcages need to be taken out to ensure each animal nestles comfortably within the other's abdominal cavity.)

The practice of stuffing animals with other animals has a long and perhaps queasy history. The Romans were past masters at this matryoshka-doll art, stuffing sheep into bears into giraffes, and in 1807 the gastronome Alexandre Grimod de la Reynière attempted to beat them at their own game with what he called his *'rôti sans pareil'*, which involved, in order, a warbler stuffed inside a bunting, inside a lark, a thrush, a quail, a lapwing, a golden plover, a partridge, a woodcock, a teal, a guinea fowl, a duck, a chicken, a pheasant, a goose, a turkey and a bustard. You'll note that in de la Reynière's order the chicken and the duck are the other way around.

Other recipes are for the 'pheduqua', a pheasant stuffed with a duck stuffed with a quail; a bustagoochiduck, a bustard stuffed with a goose stuffed with a chicken stuffed with a duck, and a woodlapwarb, a warbler inside a lapwing inside a woodcock. You can make up your own, which might form an amusing parlour game this Christmas, but please bear in mind that wild birds are protected by law under the Wildlife and Countryside Act of 1981.

18.

SING AULD LANG SYNE – ALL OF IT

On New Year's Eve we hold hands and sway and mumble our way through this tune, barely getting the first line right. Most people only attempt the first verse and first chorus, but as Robert Burns wrote it there are five verses. So, if you feel up to it, here they are:

Auld Lang Syne
Should auld acquaintance be forgot,
And never brought to mind?
Should auld acquaintance be forgot,
And auld lang syne?

CHORUS:
For auld lang syne, my jo,

For auld lang syne,
We'll tak a cup o' kindness yet,
For auld lang syne.

And surely ye'll be your pint-stowp !
And surely I'll be mine!
And we'll tak a cup o' kindness yet,
For auld lang syne.

We twa hae run about the braes,
And pulled the gowans fine;
But we've wander'd mony a weary fit,
Sin auld lang syne.

We twa hae paidl'd i' the burn,
Frae morning sun till dine;
But seas between us braid hae roar'd
Sin auld lang syne.

And there's a hand, my trusty friend!
And gie's a hand o' thine!
And we'll tak a right gude-willy waught ,
For auld lang syne.

19.

CELEBRATE THE NEW YEAR IN STYLE

Joining hands in the living room and singing 'Auld Lang Syne' is a lot of fun, but New Year's Eve is the occasion of the best free party you will ever attend.

The centre of any big city on December 31st is a riot of merrymakers, fireworks, free concerts and light shows. You can see in the New Year riding a giant goose, climbing into the air on a ferris wheel, or skating on an artificial pond (which is a great way to get to know someone on a New Year's Eve date, because it involves lots of attempts to hold one another up). It's one of the few times in the year when children are much in evidence after about 10pm (in London or New York, at least: in Rome or Seville they take a rather more enlightened attitude). When it's all over you can pile on a train at twelve thirty and be back at home tucked up by two. Some cities offer all-night transport for free. And although you'll probably have a hangover the next morning, there won't be any mess in the kitchen, nor any stained aunts asleep on the sofa.

If you want to spend some money, there are bars, clubs, pubs, restaurants and parties that are ticketed in advance, and New Year's Eve carriage rides, boating trips, burlesque shows… whatever your heart desires. It's definitely something to consider if your usual activity is listening to the radio in the kitchen with a slightly stale mince pie.

20.

BREAK YOUR NEW YEAR'S RESOLUTIONS

People will tell you that New Year's resolutions usually don't work because they tend to be too big, sweeping and ambitious, and that if you want to succeed you should make realistic resolutions which are achievable in small steps and which you can stick to. I offer instead a counsel of despair: whatever you've resolved, grandiose or piffling, abandon it on January 2nd.

New Year's resolutions fail because we don't understand the situation psychologically. What's happening is that we feel guilty for the excesses of the Christmas season and seek to punish ourselves. We try vainly to set our lives and the world right with some hasty self-imposed edicts. But the guilt wears off; the workaday world surges back. Inevitably we backslide. Then we feel bad for breaking our resolutions. Guilt engenders guilt.

I suggest you make symbolic resolutions only. On January 1st, resolve to lose weight (if that is your resolution of choice): go on a severe diet on that day. It won't be difficult, since you'll still be half-stuffed. Then on January 2nd, tuck into the remaining chocolates, cake and turducken with no feelings of guilt whatever. What a relief! Losing weight can be left to July when you need to look good for the beach. Who wants to diet in winter, when it's important to lay up fat stores? Use January 1st to remind yourself of your long-term goals so that you can put them into practice at a time when it's more convenient.

In January, gyms should offer special one-day memberships that expire on the second day of the month. Off licences should have 'welcome back' promotions. Bookshops, which would normally expect to sell more books to people who are forcing themselves to read, should lay off staff. Similarly with musical instrument manufacturers and language schools.

21.

GO TO AN OUTDOOR ICE SKATING RINK

Researchers are still struggling to understand how it is physically possible to skate on ice. In other words, why does a metal blade, dragged across the surface of a body of frozen water, not just grind to a halt? Preliminary evidence suggests that the surface few nanometres of water ice achieve a barely perceptible semi-liquid state that reduces friction. The finer points, however, are still unexplained.

In disregard of these unresolved matters, outdoor rinks open up all over the country every winter. There are small mobile touring rinks that work with generators, and seasonal rinks on a grander scale. In London, there are magnificent open rinks at Somerset House, Alexandra Palace and the Tower of London. And you can pop in to see the Crown jewels afterwards.

One tip: if you have to hire skates at the rink – and most people do this – bring some thick socks. Your skates probably won't fit exactly and your feet won't be accustomed to the heavy boots. Ill-fitting skates can cause terrible blisters that will persist for weeks. A pair of really thick socks, worn over thinner ones, will provide protection. Make sure the socks are long enough to reach up and over the sides of the boots, otherwise the sides will dig into you.

Skating is really all about socks.

22.

PLAY BANDY

As well as skating round and round in a circle, you can play all sorts of games on ice.

Rosette skating is one of the most charming. This is an ice version of 'kiss chase', in which players are numbered and given a blue rosette if a boy, and a pink rosette if a girl. Players must then try to catch a skater with a differently-gendered rosette and the same number, and pair off with them. It's popular on Valentine's Day in Finland.

Or try bandy. It's a game similar to ice hockey except that it uses a small round ball. It also predates ice hockey by several centuries. In 1913, England won the European Bandy Championships, but it's been downhill ever since.

Or there's freeze tag. Divide into two teams, each with a team captain. The captain's job is to try to tag the other team members, who must freeze in place when they are touched. Only their own team captain can unfreeze them. When all of one team are frozen, the other team wins. Captains may not be frozen.

Another simple game for kids is ice gliding. All players start at one end of the rink and take three big strides forward, after which they glide unpowered. The one to go the furthest wins.

Or try 'duck, duck, goose'. Skaters stand in a circle while one player, designated 'it', circles round, tapping each skater and calling out 'duck!' When they suddenly change tack and instead shout 'goose!', the tapped player must try to catch them, chasing them around the perimeter of the circle. If they don't manage to catch them, they become 'it' themselves.

Or make up your own game. No one has yet tried paintballing on ice, as far as I'm aware, but there may be good reasons for that.

23.

GO TOUR SKATING

… also called free skating, back-country skating or wild skating. This is skating on frozen canals, rivers and lakes for long distances (sometimes hundreds of kilometres). Tour skating is popular in the Scandinavian countries and in Canada.

Natural bodies of water often look frozen solid when they're not. So tour skating is much more risky than rink skating, and safety should come first. The chief thing to bear in mind is, rather like riding a see-saw, you should never do it alone.

If you do fall in, and for some reason your friend can't help you, you need some way of getting out, so portable spikes are indispensable. These are worn around the neck, and, if you take a plunge, you can use them to grip onto the ice and haul yourself out. You should also take a lightweight rope for hauling others out: failing to save their lives can prey on your mind afterwards. Ice poles for testing the thickness of ice are also a good idea, plus all the appropriate winter clothing (and possibly dark glasses to combat ice glare). Special skates help too. Tour skaters use long-bladed skates designed for fast, unidirectional travel.

So: not a risk-free or cost-free sport, but being out in the country, flying along in gorgeous winter conditions, will remind you of the first time you rode a bike, when with the effortless push of a foot you achieved an amazing grace and power.

24.

BUSK INDOORS

Winter is not the ideal season for outdoor busking. It's difficult to manipulate fingers and lips in the cold. But various indoor opportunities present themselves.

One is the metro system. Different metro systems have different rules, so check with the authorities first. On the London tube, for example, acolyte buskers must pass an interview in front of a panel of musicians, after which they are licensed to receive a certain number of pitches per week on a computerized booking system.

As with anywhere in the western world, the performers who predominate seem to be guys with ratty beards performing 'No Woman No Cry' over and over again, but there are many genuinely remarkable talents giving their all on melodeons, theremins, noseflutes and stylophones.

Or try in shopping centres. You will need to be

officially sanctioned, but try presenting your case to the centre manager. Be very respectful, dress like an off-duty bank assistant, and offer a complimentary copy of your CD, and they may have mercy on you.

Or try local businesses. If a café likes your act, it may book you for a spot inside. Small bars and restaurants are always looking for ways to lure in customers.

If you don't have an act, spend the winter productively: grab a noseflute and practise.

25.

GO TO AN ONSEN

An onsen is a communal bath. You sometimes find them in big cities in the West, but they are more prevalent in the Far East. At an onsen, you bathe naked with other people, usually in single-sex groups. Mixed-sex bathing is also possible.

Why bathe with other people? Well, the inhibitions of ordinary social life break down and people are open and friendly. Exteriors, real and symbolic, are divested. Everyone is equally naked. It's a childlike feeling: there is something curiously sexless about naked people.

At the more upmarket types of onsen you can bathe outdoors in natural hot springs. Drinks are sometimes served by waiters with clothes on. (At an onsen, they are clothed and you are naked, but you outrank them.) If you go in winter, as many do, it's a unique pleasure to feel the cold air caress you as your body sinks into the steaming sulphurous depths of the spring.

Each establishment has different rules, but the main one is probably 'don't get into the bath unless you have washed first'. At an onsen, you don't get in the bath to get clean, you get clean to get into the bath.

26.

SEE THE NORTHERN LIGHTS

You can see the northern lights at any time of the year from September to April, but winter is the best time, for the simple reason that the nights are longer in winter. The more night-time, the more chance of spotting the aurora borealis.

The lights are caused by the 'solar wind': electrically charged particles that stream earthwards from the sun and are funnelled by the earth's magnetic field onto the north and south poles. These particles react with gases in the atmosphere, creating a dazzling noctilucent display that has been variously described as a celestial disco and a cosmic peacock battle.

In the north, the zone in which the lights are visible sits over the Arctic in an oval that takes in Canada, Iceland, Greenland, northern Scandinavia and northern Asia; most tourists from Europe head to Iceland or Lapland on special package holidays.

There are also 'southern lights' (the aurora australis), but these are more difficult to get to and the only accommodation will be with some bemused, bearded scientists who only speak Russian.

The lights twist and move rapidly as if alive, but their rapidity and evanescence make them shortlived and unpredictable: there is no guarantee that they will put in an appearance at all. If you want to go, be prepared to enjoy yourself whatever happens, and plan to get in some ice bowling (see §30), snow tubing (see §52), tour skating (see §23), igloo building (see §91) or snowmobiling (see §43).

27.

TELL A STORY ROUND THE CAMPFIRE

As human beings we have an insatiable thirst for stories. TV stories, film stories, book stories, stories in religion and myth, campfire stories. There is nothing trivial about stories. A successful story-creator has a job for life. The demand will never run out, though the supply may occasionally exceed it. If you think about your needs you will put some sort of entertainment high on the list: food, clothing, shelter, human contact and stories.

Campfire stories probably began at the cave mouth, after the successful or unsuccessful hunt. The cavepeople needed someone to explain the success or the failure: thus the storyteller, the griot, the novelist. What does it mean to be a human and not an animal? What do animals have to teach us? What are the births, deaths, wars and suffering actually all about? Why is it important to keep trying? These answers, in the form of stories, are actually so powerful that they can make the difference between life and death, between wanting to go on and wanting to give up.

No one's saying that you need to be this high-minded. You might just want to tell a ghost story. But be aware that the chief function of a storyteller is to capture the listener's emotions, and to do this you need to resonate with them on a deeper level.

So, take a story – one you've read or made up yourself – and practise it aloud to yourself first. Tell it in your own words. Take it seriously. People respond to solemnity around a campfire. Pay attention to pacing and suspense. Withhold information. Tantalize your audience. Make sure you've got a pay-off.

As flames flicker on faces, atavistic forces are unleashed.

28.

EXPERIENCE HOT CHOCOLATE WITH A DIFFERENCE

How about hot chocolate with cheese? Or Earl Grey hot chocolate? There are so many ways of making this gorgeous wintry drink.

Take the first one, hot chocolate with cheese. This is popular in the true home of chocolate, South America, particularly Colombia, where it's called *El Chocolate Santafereño*. To make it, you need the type of salty white cheese known as *queso blanco*. Take a square of this cheese (if you can't get it, a mild feta is quite similar) and immerse it into the chocolate, where it forms a gooey sludge. Drink the chocolate down and then gulp up the salty cheese, taking a bite of some toasted bread while you do so. Delicious!

Or try hot cardomom chocolate. You can make this

yourself: buy a bar of very dark chocolate, 80% cocoa solids or more, and grate it into a saucepan. Add milk and a teaspoon of sugar. Now add two cardamom pods and bring it to a gentle simmer. Turn on the Shipping Forecast.

Chocolate doesn't have to be overpoweringly sweet. The Aztecs flavoured it with chilli and vanilla, and used it to anoint the faces, fingers and toes of newborn children.

On the other hand, you might like overpoweringly sweet chocolate. How about whipping up a cup of conventional chocolate, and then, when you serve it, floating a chocolate coin on the froth?

29.

SHOVEL SNOW FROM A PATH OR DRIVEWAY FOR SOMEONE

Shovelling snow is hard physical work. Some elderly or infirm people might not be up to it. If you can help them out, you'll be doing them a big favour.

Having said that, you need to make sure you protect yourself. Don't give yourself a heart attack. Take frequent rests. Bend and straighten properly from the knees. Don't use a spade, as this will make the job twice as long: use a proper shovel with raised sides. Bank the snow up where it won't be in the way (i.e. not on other paths or access routes). You can use grit or salt to keep the area clear but be aware of the effect on gardens: roses don't like extra salt in their diets.

Once you've done your own path and some of your elderly neighbours', a thought might come sneaking into your mind: how about charging ordinary punters?

People will pay to have snow cleared from their properties or the pavement in front of them. Small shops will also pay to have areas of the street cleared near their premises, and small shopkeepers won't have time to do the job themselves. You can service two or three houses or shops per hour easily, and charge each of them a few pounds a time.

The beauty of it is that there could be another snowfall tomorrow, and they'll have to pay again!

30.

GO ICE BOWLING AT THE ANCHORAGE FUR RENDEZVOUS

Fur Rendezvous…?

I'm glad you asked. The Fur Rendezvous (or Fur Rondy) began in the early twentieth century as a meet-up for fur trappers, and has evolved into 'the best winter carnival in the world' (according to *National Geographic*, though they may not have been to Rio). There are all sorts of events, but one of the most intriguing is ice bowling. It's also one of the easiest to copy if you happen to be unable to get to Anchorage.

Ice bowling is the same as ten-pin bowling, except played on ice. Ideally you need a frozen lake or river, but you can also use compacted snow. If the latter, find a park or cordoned-off side-street with a good covering of snow and then stamp it down hard: it'll also help if you sprinkle it with water and allow it to freeze. Make a lane by putting walls of snow on either side.

Now you need a bowling ball and some pins. On a budget, you can use a basketball and some cans or plastic bottles.

The rules are the same as ten-pin bowling, except that you're going to need someone at the far end to set the pins back up after every shot, and return the ball.

Another staple of the Fur Rondy is Outhouse Racing, in which teams race mobile lavatories on skis: this is the 'number two' most popular sport in Anchorage.

31.

PICK YOUR OWN CHRISTMAS TREE

Some farms will display cut trees; some will allow you to pick a living tree and then cut it for you; and some, most exciting of all (and closest to the Hans Christian Andersen model of Christmas), will let you choose and cut your own. Find out in advance whether you need your own saw.

Have a good look at your chosen tree to make sure it's healthy. Broken branches and brown needles are obviously not a good sign. If the tree is already cut, lift it up about a foot from the ground and let it fall heavily on its stump. If needles rain down, pass.

Get a tree with a good length of nude stump. You're going to need it to fix it in a pot, and you don't want to have to cut the lower branches off.

Trees like water. It's a mistake to leave your tree dry

in the hope that it will survive. A freshly cut tree can absorb several litres of water in the first few hours, and will continue to take up water during its sojourn in your living room. Unfortunately a pool of water near a source of electricity (Christmas tree lights) is dangerous, so you should make sure your tree is super-stable, probably by purchasing a Christmas-tree stand. Keep pets away: many Christmas tree collapses are caused by cats leaping into the branches.

Rooted or balled trees are more expensive, but it's an investment in future Christmases. The only problem (if it is a problem) is that the tree will get bigger, and may in future years fill your living room entirely, leaving no space for relatives.

32.

MAKE YOUR OWN CHRISTMAS TREE

Consider first the newspaper tree. In this, the trunk and branches are all made of rolled-up newspaper. If you fancy a go, take a number of sheets of a large-format newspaper and roll them up into a long tube. By combining sheets so that they overlap one another you can make a trunk rivalling a conventional tree in height. Tape or glue the sheets in place. Now make smaller versions to serve as branches. Affix the branches all round, longer ones at the bottom, shorter ones at the top, creating the traditional conical Christmas tree shape. Secure the whole thing on a wooden base with a pole support running up inside the trunk. A tip: it's tricky to fix branches without cutting holes in the trunk, which may weaken it; so instead support the branches at their tips with string, tethered to the top of the tree. This makes the tree collapsible if you want to store it.

Or the bottle tree. Create a superstructure from wood or plastic tubes, and fix green bottles at intervals to give a tree shape. You can put a neon tube inside the superstructure so that it lights up at the flick of a switch, casting green shadows around the room.

Or make a tree entirely of painted wood offcuts. Or of cardboard. Or of felt. Or of last year's Christmas tree, denuded and painted in bright colours. Your imagination and creativity are the only limit. And you can make a different design every year.

33.

MAKE EDIBLE CHRISTMAS TREE DECORATIONS

Now you've made your own tree, you need some home-made decorations to go with it.

There are lots of ways to do this, but one of the best is to make biscuits. Roll out some ordinary shortbread pastry – 4oz (120g) butter, 6oz (180g) plain flour, 2oz (60g) caster sugar – and make it into shapes using cutters; or if you want to be more adventurous, cut out your own shapes. When they're baked, decorate with icing (you can use food colouring with the icing for multicoloured effects). You can write messages on the biscuits with icing, or dedicate each biscuit to a particular person. Drill a hole in the top of each biscuit (you don't have to use an actual drill, but be careful or the biscuit will crumble) and attach a ribbon.

Another classic Christmas tree decoration is an

orange studded with cloves. Try it with smaller citrus fruits such as clementines. Piercing the skin with the clove spikes fills the room with a Christmassy fragrance.

Or you can take shop-bought biscuits, chocolates or sweets and hang them up. Biscuit curls can be arranged on wire or pipe cleaners to form a star for the top of the tree. Chocolates can be hung in individual boxes.

The question is, when to actually eat these goodies? You can't eat them before Christmas Day without ruining the tree, and on the day itself there will be a lot of other food competing for your gustatory attention. Nor can you wait till you take the tree down: the biscuits will be a bit stale by Twelfth Night. I'd suggest you compromise. Make the perishable decorations on Christmas Eve as a fun activity, and schedule Boxing Day as an 'eat the tree' day.

34.

STRING POPCORN FOR THE BIRDS

Another good Christmas tree decoration is to make popcorn strings. Just pop some corn and string it in long chains using a needle and thread. But it isn't really edible. After an hour or two, popcorn takes on the texture of Styrofoam. Birds will eat it, however.

In fact, you might like to decorate two trees: one for indoors and one for outdoors. The outdoor tree could be a real living tree, or last year's Christmas tree in a pot. If the latter, it will be naked and rather sorry-looking, but the birds won't care, and you are going to pretty it up anyway.

Take the strings and wind them round the tree. Now add some more things that birds like to eat in winter: some pine cones, perhaps, covered in unsalted butter or lard (birds can't process salt). Or add some pieces of fat from unsalted cuts of meat, or small cooked potatoes, cut-up apples and pears, or pieces of bread. You can also make strings of sunflower seeds or small fruits such as cranberries or blueberries. Different species go for different things: fruit is popular with starlings and tits; robins and blackbirds like cheese. Put the widest variety of household scraps on your tree and you will attract the widest range of species.

Your outside tree may outshine your inside one, given that the birds themselves are the living decorations.

35.

VOLUNTEER FOR A CHRISTMAS HOMELESS CHARITY

Thousands of people spend Christmas sleeping rough in shop doorways. Various charities exist to help.

Many of these charities offer more than just turkey and sprouts. They also provide overnight accommodation, medical and dental services, pharmacies, opticians, haircutting and manicuring, podiatry, showering facilities, and help with jobs and permanent accommodation. If you can provide any of these services, you will be warmly welcomed. Entertainers are also in high demand.

'Christmas' doesn't just mean Christmas Day: some organizations will offer services throughout the Christmas season, right up until New Year. It's often after Christmas that they need the most help, so bear this in mind when you are planning your application.

Don't wait until Christmas Day to apply: there may be an application procedure that will take a while. Start thinking about it at least a month in advance.

In the UK, the Crisis at Christmas centres are justly famous, but they are based mainly in the capital. Other charities and church groups outside London offer similar services: there is probably one in your city.

36.

GO CAROL SINGING

Many people don't open the door to carol singers. So if you want to go carol singing this year, the best tip is – don't start singing until they have opened the door!

Another tip is to go with a group – but not a big one. A small group is enough to make you feel brave, but dividing the spoils among fifteen people afterwards is a little depressing.

Of course, you're probably not doing it for base pecuniary motives.

One good idea is to have a unique selling point of some kind. A musical instrument will serve the purpose. When people open the door to someone playing a flute or a euphonium, certain Christmas-related neurones fire in their brains. With luck, they will invite you in to play at their Christmas parties. (Health and safety guidelines would warn you never to enter the houses of strangers at any time of the year, but research shows that Christmas is the jolliest time of the year to be kidnapped.)

One small point: 'Silent Night', if you're singing about it, is an oxymoron.

37.

PLANT A ROSE FOR WINTER

Roses are very hardy and can be planted in late winter with no problems at all. You can buy them by mail-order (they're very cheap), and when they arrive they are just little sticks. Here's how to give them a good start.

First, find a place in your garden that gets a good six hours of sun. Then dig a hole about 16 inches (41 cm) square and 18 inches (46 cm) deep. Get some good-quality all-purpose compost (or horse manure, if you have it) and mix it with the spoil from the hole. Place some of the mixture back in the hole so it forms a small mound at the bottom. Put your rose, roots down, onto this mound. Spread the roots out a bit so it sits astride the mound: this will give it a firmer purchase on the earth and will encourage more vigorous growth. Fill in all around the rose with the rest of the soil mixture. Ensure that the 'graft union' (the point at which the root makes its first branch) is sitting just above the soil, but not under it.

Pack the soil down firmly, give it a good watering and stand back. These roses will survive frosts (apart from severe ground frosts which freeze the earth solid) and will begin to grow shoots in spring.

38.

GET AWAY FROM THE JANUARY SALES

In a classic comic novel of the 1970s, the main character creates a chain of shops that sell rubbish. Reversing the usual custom, he holds January sales in October, in which everything doubles in price: the slogan is 'Giant Rubbish Sale: Huge Increases'. They are a roaring success.

Christmas dominates world culture, making its presence felt (pun intended) even in countries with no Christian tradition. The warm-up to Christmas and the cool-down afterwards can take almost a third of the entire passage of the earth around the sun. Retailers try to push the sales as far past the 25th of December as possible, capitalizing on the Yuletide momentum in order to get rid of their unsold stock.

Presumably, if retailers thought it would be

profitable, sales would be unending, rather like the 'permanent revolution' of Trotsky, in which things are everlastingly in reaction to a normality that has ceased to exist.

If sales were of some benefit, they would be endurable, but actually they encourage us to buy goods we don't need at some cost to our well-being. A study in 2013 found that the stress brought on by seasonal bargain-hunting led to raised blood pressure not experienced at other times of the year.

With this is mind, perhaps the best you can hope for is to go to Belgium. In this enlightened country, the state regulates all sales and they are time-limited to a period of one month.

39.

CELEBRATE VALENTINE'S DAY

Valentine's Day is the celebration of everything pink, quilted and fluffy, a hymn to spring and young love – which is odd, because it happens in the dead of winter. You will have to tramp through freezing slush to deliver a Valentine's card.

Actually, there is some evidence that Valentine's Day was originally later in the year: Chaucer in his poem *Parliament of Fowles* puts the day at a time 'when every bird cometh to choose his mate' (presumably in spring) and in the Eastern Orthodox church the date of the veneration of St Valentine (the Roman priest who was imprisoned and fell in love with the jailer's daughter) is in July. In Carnival-celebrating countries Valentine's Day also falls at other times of the year, because a Valentine's Day of 14 February is too close to the season for semi-naked parading, and gets lost in the noise.

And if you're Welsh, and you celebrate St Dwynwen's Day, the traditional day of lovers, then that's on January 25th. This is even further into the dead of winter, which may say something about competitive masochism in Celtic cultures.

There is one Valentine's Day tradition from the Far East that Western men might like to adopt. On Valentine's Day in Korea and Japan, women are expected to give chocolates and presents, but men are not expected to return the favour. A month later, if they wish, on March 14 ('White Day'), they can respond, but hopefully by then she will have forgotten.

40.

GO SKIING

Skiing was invented in the Palaeolithic era, so it can claim to be one of the world's oldest pastimes. Stone-carvings from Rødøy in Norway, dated to around 5000BC, show a human figure standing on a pair of long planks with upturned ends that really can't be anything other than skis.

So from the earliest times skiing has been used as used as a mode of conveyance, or even in warfare (skiing soldiers in Norway were known as 'birchlegs'). Skiing as a sport is rather more recent: bronzed types in goggles began swooshing down mountains some time in the mid-19th century.

Nowadays skiing has many dozens of subcategories. There is basic downhill (or Alpine) skiing, but also ski flying (an extreme version of ski jumping), ski mountaineering, slalom skiing, heli-skiing (off-trail skiing accessed by helicopter), freestyle and stunt skiing, Telemark skiing (using a special form of ski boot which is only fixed at the toe), cross-country skiing, skijoring (skiing with a dog team; see §42), and many others.

The best place to get started in skiing, if you don't live next to a mountain, is probably your nearest dry ski slope. Taking lessons will build your confidence and greatly reduce your chances of having an accident.

On the other hand if you are determined to try heli-skiing you probably don't care too much about accidents.

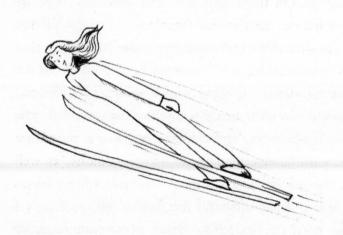

41.

GO SNOWBOARDING

If skiing doesn't appeal, perhaps snowboarding will. The two are culturally rather different.

In snowboarding, you slide down your mountain of choice on a long, flat board with a rounded nose and tail. On this board, much as with skis, there are two fixtures for the snowboarder's boots, except that on snowboards they are set transverse to the direction of travel, making the stance rather similar to that of a skateboarder. In fact, snowboarding was directly inspired by skateboarding, which is where all the trouble came in. The two sports share a subculture of youthful irreverence and street fashions, as well as many jumps and stunts – ollies, nollies, fakies, shifties – that often involve balancing or riding on obstacles. In the 1980s, when snowboarding really started taking off, skiing resorts, full of people still trying to emulate David Niven or Princess Grace of

Monaco, were outraged by this behaviour and either refused to accept snowboarders or gave them their own segregated routes, claiming, among other things, that snowboarders removed too much snow from the slopes.

Now, however, the quarrel has vanished and the two groups get on perfectly well. This is largely due to the fact that snowboarding is a multi-million dollar industry with an international following, and has become an official Winter Olympic sport. Subcultural utterances such as 'shred the gnar' are still made, but are widely tolerated.

42.

GO SLED-DOG RACING

This is not the cheapest winter hobby, because you do need to buy a sled, plus your snowgear and a dog-team. But you can always watch.

Sled-dog racing is popular in countries with substantial winters, such as Canada, the USA, the Scandinavian countries and Russia. It involves teams of four, six, eight or more dogs pulling sleds, with each sled steered by a musher. The distances involved can be very long: up to 1,200 miles in the case of the longest race, the Iditarod Trail in Alaska, which follows the route of the famous 'serum run' to Nome. The various types of racing include skijoring (from the Norwegian *skikjøring*, or 'ski driving'), in which the musher travels behind on skis; *pulka*, in which the musher rides a toboggan; *bikejoring*, in which the dogs pull a bike; scootering, in which they pull a scooter; and canicross, in which the musher merely runs along behind (and in which the distances are considerably shorter). All are brought together under the umbrella of the International Federation of Sled-dog Sports, whose stated aim is 'to encourage mushing at all levels.'

There are around 1,000 events held every year in various locations throughout the world, and you don't even need snow to take part. 'Mushing Inca Style' is an event held in Peru, where the lack of snow means that racing usually takes place on the beach.

43.

GO SNOWMOBILING

Or you could try snowmobile riding, which is the same thing but without the yelping.

Snowmobiles are small, fast vehicles with two skis at the front and a caterpillar track underneath. They are extremely tough (you can do acrobatics in them and land without pinging bolts) and versatile, and although they are designed for snow, they can run over land or even over water: if the engine is kept running at high speed they will skim over the surface. Snowmobile riding can be pursued recreationally, or as a sport called Snocross by people wearing body armor, helmets and shin guards. If you don't fancy Snocross you can try Hillcross, Watercross or the much-feared Extreme Ice series.

Snowmobiling is controversial because of the noise and potential damage to wildlife it causes. It can also be dangerous. Every year in snowmobilophile countries such as the USA and Canada there are injuries and fatalities from hitting hidden obstacles such as rocks, logs or barbed wire fences, and the activities of off-route freeriders – also called 'ditchbangers' because they follow the lines of snow-covered ditches alongside roads – are notorious. A popular sport in some parts of the snowmobiling community is stunt-riding by hurdling over roads.

44.

SEE A NATIVITY PLAY

Nativity plays have been performed for many centuries (St Francis of Assisi is said to have invented the nativity play in the 13th century, using real farm animals), but nowadays the place you are most likely to see a nativity play is at a primary school. The audience is usually made up of parents, but some nativity plays will also admit relatives and church members, so if you're not a parent you may be able to squeeze in.

The standard cast is of Mary, Joseph, the baby Jesus (usually a doll), the Wise Men, the Angel Gabriel, the shepherds and animals. However, in 2012 a serious blow was dealt to the traditional nativity play when Pope Benedict XVI declared in his autobiography that there were no farm animals present at Christ's birth: that aspect of the incarnation, he suggested, was a 'myth'. He poured a further bucket of cold water over the proceedings by declaring that the

Angels did not sing to the shepherds – a tradition that inspired Christmas carolling – but merely 'spoke'. (He added that this need not discourage anyone from representing farm animals or singing carols if they so desired.)

Nativity plays leave a lasting effect on small minds, especially if they happen to be cast in one of the lead roles. An study has yet to be undertaken on the correlation between playing Mary – the star part – and career success in later life; similarly the possible negative consequences of playing a donkey have not been explored. And is a wise man in a nativity play more likely to be a judicious in later life?

45.

GO TO A SANTACON

Otherwise known as a 'Santa convention'. Essentially this involves dressing up as Santa and then going to a place where there are dozens, hundreds or even thousands of other people dressed as Santa, and having a good time. It's more popular than you might imagine: much, much more popular. As I write, there are currently well over 300 scheduled SantaCons in nearly 40 countries in the weeks before Christmas.

Sometimes the Santas, once convened, don't behave with the benevolence and 'ho ho ho'-ing goodwill that is conventionally required of them. In fact, Santa gatherings are often associated with disorder, drunkenness, sexual display and even mild rioting, and the wilder type of SantaCons are also known as 'Santa rampages', 'Santarchy', 'Santa sedition' or 'the running of the Santas'. In Auckland, New Zealand, in 2005, in one of the most serious incidents, a mob of drunken Santas left a trail of destruction through the city, smashing shop windows, assaulting security guards and urinating from road bridges. A spokesman for the Santas later claimed it was a protest against the commercialisation of Christmas.

Other Santa events have a charitable purpose, such as the Santa pub-crawl held every year in the town of Wollonggong, Australia, where many thousands of participants (4,500 at the last count) dress up as Santa, become horribly drunk and raise money for the Salvation Army (which, of course, promotes complete abstinence).

46.

TAKE UP INDOOR ROWING

The river's iced up, so there isn't really any choice. But this is to mistake the nature of indoor rowing. Bizarrely, the majority of indoor rowers have never sat in a boat. Indoor rowing is detached from outdoor rowing, and has its own rules, distances, events, world records and sporting heroes. And no-one ever moves forward a millimetre.

The early rowing machines were made with a bicycle wheel and a wooden handle. Things have changed. The latest machines are the Concept2 ergometers, each with a PC display and, in competition, a link to a master computer. Championship 'races' are held over a variety of distances, but 2,000 metres is the most common, with distance given as a readout on the display. Rowers will sometimes be in the same room, but often they will be in different rooms, or different countries. Mediated by the internet, races can take place in real time in multiple locations throughout the globe.

Indoor racing is one of the most carefully segregated of all sports, particularly when it comes to age categories. Championship races are held in five-year age bands, from 25-29 or 50-55, for example. The top age category is 95-99, though this might merely involve one very lonely woman racing against herself.

47.

BECOME A GALANTHOPHILE

The 'galanthus' is the Latin name for the snowdrop. This humble flower inspires enormous devotion, even mania on the scale of tulip and orchid frenzies. Obsessive collectors, growers and spotters, of which there are many, are known as galanthophiles.

Why the snowdrop? After all, it's a rather undistinguished little flower: low, white and modestly drooping. The appeal is the time it appears. Snowdrops are the first flowers to bloom every year, sometimes even right in the middle of winter's worst excesses. Snowdrops can appear as early as January, literally poking up through ice and snow. They are gallant little galanthi. They can be very numerous, in pearlescent carpets covering the floors of woodlands, or alternatively in little mournful clumps at the base of trees. If they had to compete with daffodils, bluebells or other spring flowers, they wouldn't seem so remarkable, but for a few short weeks snowdrops have the stage to themselves.

Galanthus Nivalus is probably the best-known variety – the familiar pure-white flower – but there are many others. The galanthus 'green tear', with green flowers, first discovered in the Netherlands, is especially prized.

To be a true galanthophile you should aim to grow your own. The bad news is that bulbs change hands for large sums, with really rare specimens going for hundreds of pounds.

48.

FORCE BULBS

If snowdrops don't satisfy your bulb mania, there are certain other options.

Bulb-forcing is the practice of taking bulbs, such as daffodil, tulip, hyacinth and narcissus, and tricking them into thinking it is spring. You do this by planting them early, under special conditions.

In order for bulbs to root and flower, they need to think they have been through a cold period that has then given way to a warm period. To achieve this, the bulbs must be 'cold-treated' first. You can buy pre-treated bulbs for forcing at garden centres, or you can cold-treat your own. If you want to try the latter, start in November. First pot up the bulbs, digging a shallow hole in some soil and inserting the bulb with the tip protruding and the root pointing downwards. Now put them in a cold, dark place for several weeks (around twelve weeks for small bulbs, fifteen weeks for larger), such as a garage or even the fridge – just make sure they don't freeze. After this time, take them out and inspect them for roots. As soon as you see roots protruding from underneath the pot, they are ready to be transferred to a warmer environment. A cool, dim place indoors is good until shoots begin to develop, after which they can be transferred to a bright windowsill, though not one above a radiator. The bulbs think spring has arrived and react accordingly.

In short, with a little forethought, this winter you could be sitting indoors in a paradise of narcissi, while the land outside remains barren.

49.

KEEP A CARP

Poles don't eat goose for Christmas; neither do Czechs tuck into turkey. In these countries, as well as in other parts of Europe, carp is the centrepiece of the Christmas dinner.

The carp is traditionally bought live and kept in a tank or bucket – often in the family bathtub – until the moment of dispatch. The head of the household, or anyone not squeamish, takes the carp (a substantial fish up to a couple of feet long), gives it a swift knock on the head and dresses it for dinner. It is served filleted and fried with various side dishes: beetroot soup and ravioli in Poland, potato salad in the Czech Republic, and shots of vodka everywhere. The bits of the carp that are surplus to requirements, such as the head and tail, are made into a nourishing Christmas soup.

Where to get a carp? Well, Eastern Europeans get them from street vendors. Come December, hundreds of these appear offering live fish for sale. Some vendors will kill the fish for you, but it's essentially a live trade – hence the bathtub.

If you don't live in Poland, Croatia, Austria, etc., getting a carp needn't be a problem. There are hundreds of Polish shops in the UK who are happy to source carp, and some mainstream supermarkets have started selling carp in the run-up to Christmas. Generally, however, they're not live. Unless you are a fisherman (with an angling license), it's going to be difficult to obtain one for your bath.

50.

MAKE A SNOW JUMP

You need a good heavy snowfall for this.

First of all, shovel your snow into a pile, about person-height, and pack it down firmly. This will be easier if you have a few people to help you. Next, create a slide down one face of this hill. You can do this by repeatedly sliding down it, making a groove, or by digging a channel with banks either side. Spray water on it to make it icy.

It's a good idea to make steps on the other side of the hill. You can do this just by carving out steps in the snow. You'll probably want to make the stepped face shorter and steeper than the slope side, which should be long and graceful.

Now you've got a snow hill that you can slide down on snowboards, tea-trays, sledges or anything else. But to make it more fun, create a snow jump. You can do this by piling up another heap of snow a few metres from the snow slide. When you come down the first hill, you travel along the ground at speed and then hit the second hill (a bit like in a skateboarding park). Build the second hill like the first except in reverse, with the sliding face going up instead of down. The second hill should be smaller, and on the far side have a sheer drop. That way you go up and over and into the air, coming down with a thump (hopefully right side up).

51.

CREATE A DEN

What is a den? It's a retreat from the world, a place where one can hunker down and revert to a more primordial state.

Children love dens made of upturned sofas and old bedspreads, or stepladders and curtains, but that's just one form of den. A den may be made of branches and tarpaulin in a forest (a bender is a type of den), or high up in a tree with a look-out platform. It may occupy an entire room and have a pool table or home cinema in it. A den may be wall-to-wall with forbidden tomes, the refuge of a bibliomaniac in a bibliophobic household.

Decorations? Well, thick hangings are recommended, and soft furnishings into which one can sink. One can be businesslike in a den, with a desk and wall-charts, but such things are not really in the right spirit. Cushions and rich fabrics made for indolence are the most den-like: an Ottoman feel is optimum. An odalisque might not go amiss.

A key aspect of dens is their size: smallness, constriction and intimacy make the best dens. A den is best with a friend. Trapped willingly in this soft, private space, things can happen which would be impossible elsewhere: plots can be plotted, friendships forged and secrets swapped.

Or you can just read a book on your own. Or write a book. In a den, time slows and the world outside fades away. In that stillness, fantasies breed.

52.

GO SNOW TUBING

Snow tubing is a sport similar to sledding, only using a gigantic inner tube as a vehicle. Because most of us don't have giant tractors to fix, snow tubing is usually only possible at outdoor activity centres during the winter months.

The mode of operations is to drag your doughnut-shaped tube up to the top of a hill (sometimes this is achieved via a mechanical winch) and sit with your bottom in the hole of the doughnut, your arms and legs splaying out at the sides. Gravity then does the rest. Tubes designed for tubing will usually have handles to grip onto and a membrane underneath to stop your bottom getting snow-burn.

A common practice is to tube in a bunch, like free-fall parachuters. This is more fun, mainly because of the screams, but also because the tube-group rotates in unpredictable ways as it goes downhill. 'Unpredictable' is the key word with snow tubing. Skiers and sledders have a modicum of control, but as soon as you get into a tube, you are more or less at its mercy. The shape of a tube and its low friction means that it can reach considerable speeds, and these factors make snow tubing a pretty lawless pursuit. As a result responsible snow-tubing is usually carried out on a separate slope with banks or rails to keep tubers in check.

53.

OBSERVE THE QUINTILLION TYPES OF SNOW

As anyone who has tried staring very intently at snow will tell you, it's very hard to actually see a snowflake. What we experience as individual 'flakes' are usually aggregates of many snowflakes. Aggregates can be so big – as much as two or three inches wide – that they flop down with audible thumps.

It is possible to see individual snowflakes with the naked eye, but to truly appreciate them you need a microscope. An ordinary school microscope will do. The trick is to get the equipment to a low temperature. Chill your slides first in a freezer, then place the microscope near an open window during a snowfall (or outside if it's water-resistant). Put a couple of slides out in the open and wait for a snowflake to land. Then transfer your catch to the microscope, without covering with a top slide, and observe under low magnification.

What you will see will depend on a lot of factors. A snowflake forms as a tiny crystal lattice high up in the freezing winter sky. As it grows, this lattice forms a hexagonal prism, which begins to develop branches, or dendrites, at its corners. Because each snowflake contains many quintillions of water molecules, no two, at the atomic level, are ever alike. Each dendrite develops at its own pace, and as the snowflake is whirled about in different temperatures and humidities, does not grow with perfect symmetry. Snowflakes, in fact, are very rarely symmetrical, adding a further layer to their complexity.

One of the earliest snowflake-observers was Johannes Kepler, who considered giving one to his friend as a Christmas present: 'the very thing for a mathematician to give since it comes down from heaven and looks like a star.'

54.

MAKE SCANDINAVIAN ICE CANDLES

For this one, it helps if the weather is cold enough to make an Inuit blench. Alternatively, you can use a chest freezer.

First of all get a bucket, or any large cylindrical container. Fill it with water and stand it outside in the freezing cold (or in your freezer). Wait for around 24 hours. The surface of the bucket should have developed a carapace of ice, perhaps an inch or more thick.

What you can't see is that the bucket will have frozen all down the sides as well, and a little along the bottom, creating a hollow ice cylinder filled with water. All you need to do now is to extract this cylinder. Do this by simply bringing the bucket indoors into a warm room, and leaving it to stand for a while. The sides will begin to melt, freeing the candle. Now take the bucket outside, turn it over, and hey presto, a hollow cylinder of ice will pop out.

Stand the ice cylinder on end, so that the top is now the base. You'll notice that the bottom has frozen a bit too, though not as much as the top (ice freezes from the top down): you can open this up a bit with a knife, if you've a mind.

Put a tea light or candle inside, light and stand back. Ghostly flickering light now illuminates the ice from within. Put it out on your steps or porch, or have it inside as a table decoration – with a goodly basin to catch the meltwater.

55.

MAKE MINCE PIES WITH REAL MINCE

It's strange, really, but mince pies did actually use to contain mince. Ingredients included minced goose, mutton or calf's tongue, mixed with suet, dried fruits and spices. There is an element of kitchen sink to mince pies (see the section on Christmas pudding, §63). And the original mince pies weren't the dainty little objects they are now: they were, in fact, proper pies, to serve to many people. They represented a main-course item rather than a dessert. The small, sweet mince pie is a twentieth-century phenomenon, a distant echo of a meatier past.

Having experimented, I can tell readers that mince pies made with real mince aren't actually too bad. The secret is to not to go too heavy on the meat, and be generous with the fruits and suet, so that it's not a meat pie, as such, but a savoury-sweet combination pie. (Standard sweet mince often contains animal suet, after all.)

Try this recipe for your mincemeat: 8oz (230g) of ground beef; 4oz (115g) beef suet; 8oz (230g) mixed raisins, sultanas or currants; 3 oz (85g) chopped dates, 2 oz (55g) muscovado sugar; 2 oz (55g) candied peel; 2 oz (55g) chopped walnuts, a couple of hard pears or apples, chopped finely; the zest and juice of a lemon; a teaspoon of mixed spice; two tablespoons of brandy or whiskey. Stir together thoroughly. This should make enough for about twenty-five small pies (we'll stick with the little pies in their foil tins). Put the mincemeat in a pastry filling of your choice and bake, gas mark 5, for about 20-25 minutes.

Real meat mince pies can still be served as a sweet, with cream or custard as usual, but rum butter or brandy butter is a better choice, complimenting the rich flavour of the meat.

56.

BATTLE WITH ORANGES

Picture the scene: a swarming crowd of men wearing medieval costumes, uttering savage cries, assault an open wagon in which a dozen men are seemingly fighting for their lives. The air is thick with curses and... oranges. Yes, there is pith aplenty, for this is the annual Battle of the Oranges in the northern Italian city of Ivrea.

The tradition is hundreds of years old and the story goes that at one point a lustful duke tried to exercise his *droit de seigneur* and have carnal knowledge of a miller's daughter on the night before her wedding. She refused him; and when he tried to press his point, she cut his head off. The citizens, in support of the miller's daughter, assaulted the duke's troops and drove him from power. The oranges represent the stones and projectiles that the citizens used – or perhaps the duke's head. The men riding in wagons represent the duke's troops.

If you want to go along, it happens in February just before Lent every year. Tourists can take part, but observers are encouraged to stand well back, because deliberate exposure to orange-related injury may not be covered by your traveller's insurance. To be spared the most zestful attentions of the *aranceri*, or Orangemen, non-combatants are advised to wear a red hat.

There is one problem with throwing oranges in the North of Italy: oranges don't grow there, it's too cold. Around a quarter of a million kilograms of oranges have to be specially imported every year from Sicily.

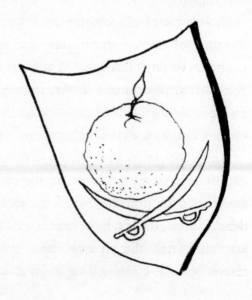

57.

CLIMB A WALL

Winter is a time to start climbing the walls. Not in frustration, you understand. In pursuit of rock-climbing glory. Indoor rock-climbing is perfect when it's too cold and wet to go out and clamber over the real thing.

Indoor rock walls are artificial surfaces that offer a series of holds, protrusions and indentations to create a vertical challenge. They are widespread at fitness gyms, sports and activity centres. There are also mobile 'touring' walls that visit public places and offer ordinary punters a go. It's easy to get involved.

Holds will often be colour-coded, with each colour signifying a particular route up the rock-face. Routes are graded by difficulty, so that holds in one colour denote a beginner's level, and holds in another an advanced level. You pick your way up following your chosen colour. Climbers are held in a harness at all times, making it a very safe sport. For extra safety you can climb in pairs ('belay buddies') or teams. Racing up a wall is not recommended, though.

Climbing is a great form of exercise for arms, legs, abdominal muscles, backs and shoulders: it brings the whole body into play, in fact, improving balance and strength.

58.

GO TO A CARNIVAL

Carnival season is between Christmas and Lent in the Christian calendar. Most carnivals, however, are held in February. Carnival is at its most elaborate and unbridled in Catholic countries such as Spain, Mexico, Italy and elsewhere, but carnivals are also held in Orthodox or Protestant countries such as Greece or Denmark. The carnival season ends on Shrove Tuesday (in the UK, Pancake Day), or, if in New Orleans, on *Mardi Gras* ('Fat Tuesday', the same day). The original idea seems to have been to use up the last remaining scraps of food before the Lenten season, but human ingenuity and love of a good time seem to have taken over.

Typical carnivalling behaviour involves outlandish and magnificent costumes, masking, parades, sporting competitions, dancing, feasting and licentiousness of all types and varieties: the most famous masked carnival is probably in Venice, but there are many other strange and startling carnival traditions from around the world. In Beuel, Germany, for example, in commemoration of the 'Washerwomen's revolt' of 1824, women are given licence to cut off the ties of any man they meet in the street. In Solsona, Spain, stuffed donkeys are suspended from a bell-tower, and the donkeys are made to urinate on the screaming populace below by means of a water pump. In Tyrnavor, Greece, the populace parade with giant papier-mâché phalluses.

Many of the most dazzling carnivals round the world are given the official UNESCO designation of Masterpieces of the Oral and Intangible Heritage of Humanity, or, in layman's terms, a Great Excuse for a Party. If you feel somewhat lugubrious during the winter months, get on a train. There is a quite enormous shindig happening somewhere very near you.

59.

SEE THE TRAFALGAR SQUARE CHRISTMAS TREE

The Christmas tree in Trafalgar Square has a remarkable story. In 1940 the Nazis overran Norway, and the Norwegian government and royal family were forced into exile in London. Britain became a vital rallying-point for the Norwegian resistance, and Norwegian troops fought alongside the British until victory in 1945. In 1947, in recognition of this assistance, the restored Norwegian government pledged to supply, every year in perpetuity, a gigantic Norwegian spruce for display in Trafalgar Square. In the presence of various dignitaries, it is cut in a snowy November forest while children sing carols. Then it is taken by sea to London, arriving in early December. It is decorated in simple Norwegian style, with long vertical strings of white lights, and the lights are switched on comparatively late, on the first Thursday of December (by contrast, most other Christmas decorations are formally switched on a month or so earlier). Again there is much ceremony and crowds of thousands of people.

At the base of the tree a sign reads: 'This tree is given by the city of Oslo as a token of Norwegian gratitude to the people of London for their assistance during the years 1940-45.'

The Trafalgar Square tree is also particularly associated with charity carol concerts, which are held every night all through December.

On Twelfth Night, the tree is taken down and recycled.

60.

ELECT A LORD OF MISRULE

… which you can do on Twelfth Night. Twelfth Night is the night of the twelfth day of Christmas, and falls (in most traditions) on the 5th of January.

What is the significance of Twelfth Night? Well, it's the day before Epiphany, which is celebrated almost as fervently as Christmas in some European nations. It also heralds the carnival season (see §58) that leads all the way to the beginning of Lent. One of the elements of the Twelfth Night celebrations in former times was the election of a Lord of Misrule, perhaps inspired by the Roman festival of Saturnalia (see §81).

The Lord and Lady of Misrule were elected by means of a pie that contained a bean and a pea. Whoever got the bean was the Lord and whoever got the pea was the Lady. (If a bean was discovered by a female she had to give it to the man sitting on her left, and similarly if a male discovered a pea.)

Until midnight, their commands had to be followed to the letter. Much social upheaval could result: acts of mild revenge in which pillars of the community were forced to scrub floors were not uncommon. At the stroke of midnight, the Lord and Lady would revert to their humble degree, and presumably take whatever consequences had flowed from their actions. Shakespeare in his *Twelfth Night*, probably written for the Twelfth Night revels of 1602, took this topsy-turvydom as his theme, particularly in the figure of Malvolio, a servant who thinks, in his cross-gartered pomposity, that he can become a nobleman.

Following one elected person's commands can make for an entertaining evening. Different people react in different ways, some becoming drunk with power, others indecisive and forbearing.

61.

WATCH FROGS SPAWNING

Winter is the breeding season for frogs and toads. They will breed any time from January to April, and the fertilized eggs will hatch as tadpoles in spring.

'Spawning', 'breeding', 'mating' and 'egg-laying' all refer essentially to the same activity. When conditions are right, male and female frogs get together, sometimes in single pairs, other times in large groups of mixed males and females. The individuals may pair off in a phenomenon known as 'amplexus', in which a male mounts a female and grips her tightly (which must be very difficult to do): this is not copulation, however, but 'pseudocopulation', since no internal fertilization takes place. During mass spawning events, females emit eggs, which are then fertilized externally by the males. So what looks like breeding is in fact simultaneously breeding and egg-laying: there is no gestation period.

Toads spawn slightly later in the year. (Frogs and toads are easy to distinguish from one another. Frogs have smooth skins with a distinctive patch behind the eye, and move in jumps. Toads have warty skins, are generally larger, and crawl. Their eggs are different too. Frog spawn is laid in clumps, whereas toad spawn is laid in strings.)

A mass spawning, also known as a spawning 'frenzy', is a very lively and noisy event, with frogs clambering over one another to find the best spot, emitting loud purring croaks. Their blank expressions and staring eyes make their single-minded enthusiasm all the more amusing.

62.

IMBIBE A WINTER ALE

Come December, pubs are full of hearty types sinking dark brown pints. These concoctions are 'winter ales' or 'winter warmers'. They are a seasonal phenomenon which the above-mentioned types would probably regard with grave suspicion at any other time of the year, and make their appearance in pubs as guest ales, or in off-licences as transitory bottled beers.

Winter ales are rather difficult to define. They are darker than ordinary ales, with a reddish or brownish tint. They are not brown ales, which have a characteristic nutty flavour high in tannins. Winter ales tend to be higher in alcohol than either brown ales or ordinary ales – thus their 'warming' quality. Neither should winter ales be confused with stouts, which are much darker (particularly the familiar Irish stout, with its strong note of coffee), and not true ales at all. Winter ales may have chocolate notes: a popular winter ale malt is known as a 'chocolate malt'. Other flavours will include vanilla and cinnamon.

So: stronger, darker and maltier than ordinary beer, with a suggestion of spices and stables. This is the essence of a winter ale.

Non-beer-lovers can enjoy the names, with their wintery themes: Hibernation Ale, Harpoon, Twelve Dogs of Christmas, Wintervention, Snowed In, Cabin Fever, Abominable Ale, Ill-Tempered Gnome and Hell Hath no Fury, which has a label featuring a woman giving a severe-dressing down to an apologetic devil.

63.

MAKE A CHRISTMAS PUDDING WITH BEER

The traditional English Christmas pudding is served *flambé*, uniquely among English dishes. It is also, traditionally, spherical, and contains so much alcohol that it looks like a flaming cannonball.

Because of the preserving qualities of the alcohol, Christmas puddings, like Christmas cake, can be made well in advance of Christmas Day itself. The most traditional approach is to make a pudding on the 25th Sunday after Trinity, which falls some time in late November. Each member of the household should have a chance to stir the mixture and make a wish. Then, various talismans are added: sixpences (in former times), wishbones and other silver or metal objects. The person who finds a talisman can keep it. Nowadays pound coins are a good alternative.

Christmas pudding recipes are complex and vary widely. The main ingredients tend to be flour, treacle, dark brown sugar (the latter two of which give the pudding its dark colour), dried fruits such as currants, raisins, apricots, cherries and dates, nuts, butter, eggs, ginger, spices and breadcrumbs. To make a beer-soaked Christmas pudding, take all the dried fruits and soak them overnight in beer (bitter, not lager, and preferably a winter ale). The final ingredient is of course the spirituous liquors: rum, brandy and whiskey. Copious amounts are added to the mix, and then, after the pudding is cooked and is resting in storage, 'fed' to the parched pudding to keep it tipsy.

Traditionally, puddings are boiled in a pudding cloth rather than a bowl (giving the spherical shape). The most famous description of a Christmas pudding is in Charles Dickens' *A Christmas Carol*, where he focuses on the smell: 'like an eating-house and a pastrycook's next door to each other, with a laundress's next door to that.'

Only English cooking could smell of washing and still be held in high esteem.

64.

HURL A SILVER BALL

If you happen to be in Cornwall this winter, you can take part in a tradition that dates back many centuries. It's called Hurling the Silver Ball. It takes place only in three locations: St Columb, St Ives and Bodmin. The St Columb hurling is held on Shrove Tuesday (which usually falls in February) and on the second Saturday following it; the St Ives tournament is held on Feast Monday, which is in early February; and the Bodmin hurling is held as part of the Beating the Bounds ceremony every five years (date variable). It's mainly local residents who take part, but there are always plenty of spectators.

Hurling is played with a small ball, about the size of a cricket ball, made of apple-wood coated with silver, and usually inscribed with a motto, such as: 'Town and Country do your best, for in this parish I must rest.' Two teams try to get this projectile to one of two points two miles apart, or across the parish boundary. There are no fixed rules, and the shopkeepers board up the town's glass the night before the game. Various injuries and even a fatality have been recorded.

After the licensed mayhem is over, the player who has scored the winning goal tours the town's pubs, dipping the silver ball into tankards of beer and christening them 'silver beer'. The winner can keep the ball if he wishes, though he must pay for a replacement with a price tag in the range of £300.

65.

CELEBRATE PONGAL

Pongal is another winter festival. It takes place in early January and is a harvest festival sacred to the Tamils of southern India and Sri Lanka. It's also known as Thai Pongal, not because it has anything to do with Thailand, but because 'Thai' is the name of the month in which Pongal takes place.

Now, you probably can't go to Chennai or Pondicherry to celebrate Pongal. But there may well be Tamil communities near you who would appreciate your knowing something about it; it's a festival on the scale of Christmas, after all.

Pongal lasts for four days. The first day is devoted to family gatherings and to the decoration of the house with designs called *kolam*, brightly-coloured geometric shapes executed in chalk. On the second day, a dish, also called Pongal, is prepared, consisting of sweet rice flavoured with cardamoms and other spices. The pot is expected to boil over, since Pongal actually means a 'boiling over' or 'abundance'. The proper reaction to the boiling-over is to shout 'Pongal o-Pongal!' On the third day, cows are venerated by being garlanded and having their horns painted, and in rural areas the custom of jallikattu is practised, in which young men compete to retrieve money bags tied to the horns of ferocious bulls. This, being highly dangerous, gives rise to disapproving newspaper headlines every year. Girls practise the slightly more pacific sport of feeding crows with balls of coloured rice. On the fourth day, brothers give presents to their married sisters to show them that marriage has its compensations, and the festival ends with firework displays, open-air concerts, singing and dancing.

66.

SEE THE WINTER'S TALE

This is the play with the famous line 'Exit, pursued by a bear'. It's not known whether Shakespeare used a real bear; there would have been a plentiful supply of bears in Jacobean London due to the popularity of bear-baiting, but it might have been tricky to train a bear to pursue an actor stage left without also eating him.

The Winter's Tale is one of Shakespeare's last three major plays (along with *Cymbeline* and *The Tempest*), written around 1610. It's sometimes called a 'problem play', but that's mainly because of its unusual structure: it starts off like a tragedy and ends up like a comedy, with a happy ending. In fact, the ending is so happy it's almost a parody of a happy ending. (I won't ruin it for you if you haven't seen it, but it involves a miracle with a statue.) It's all gloriously improbable, and the title reflects the fact: a 'winter's tale' was a tale told by a fireside in winter when it was too cold to go out. The title's really saying: 'gather round, I'm going to tell you something incredible'.

If you can't catch a performance there are several film versions. Stoke up the fire, settle onto the sofa and suspend disbelief.

67.

MAKE LINOCUT CHRISTMAS CARDS

If you generally buy cheap flimsy cards with hideous illustrations, in packs of a thousand, then making your own linocut cards is probably not going to save you money. Even so, it isn't expensive, and once you've purchased the kit – which can be done for about the price of a hardback book – you'll never need to do it again.

'Linocut' refers to the technique of cutting designs on small squares of linoleum, which can then be used for printing. Craft shops can supply the linoleum squares, plus the other things you need: linoleum cutters, ink and a roller.

The method is simple. Draw a design on the lino and then cut away those portions that will appear white in the finished design. Now prepare some card blanks out of a good card stock, preferably something absorbent: again, a craft shop will be able to advise you. Now roll the ink on the lino. When you do so, only the uncarved areas will receive colour. Turn the inked lino onto the card and press it down with the back of a spoon (sold separately). Hey presto, a card is born. If you want to make it a bit more complex, use two designs of different colours and overprint them, allowing for drying time between printings.

Handmade linocut cards are wonderful things to make and to get. They're thoughtful and Christmassy. And you can write your own personal messages inside.

68.

TRY ICE FISHING

For this activity you need a few things that you don't need for regular fishing. The first is a short pole: you won't need to cast out. The second is some safety equipment to get yourself out of the water if you fall in (see the section on tour skating, §23). The third is an auger, for drilling the hole. Augers are either hand-turned or mechanically turned. You can buy ice-augers by mail order or at fishing shops.

Ice that is at least four inches (10cm) thick is a must. You are going to be standing on it and performing little dances of joy on it when you catch a fish, so it has to bear your weight. To judge the quality of the ice, bear this old saying in mind: 'Thick and blue, tried and true. Thin and crispy, way too risky.'

When you come to dig the hole, choose a place over deepish water where there are reputed to be a lot of fish in the unfrozen months. Sink a bore-hole, then widen it out by chipping the ice at the sides. You'll need a hole big enough to pull a fish through: unless you happen to be on a lake famed for its monster carp, a few inches in diameter should do. Bait with anything colourful that will catch the eye of a sluggish seasonally depressed fish.

Fishing is a sedentary sport marked by long periods of inactivity and meditation on failed marriages. This can lead you to freeze solid if you don't take appropriate winter clothing, a hat and a thermos flask with some hot chocolate.

Don't start a big fire on the ice to cook your catch.

69.

GO ICE BOATING

To get to a choice spot for ice-fishing, you might consider ice boating. This is a recreation like ordinary boating, except the boat is designed to glide over ice.

An ice boat is superficially like an ordinary sailboat, but underneath the hull are runners with sharp blades like ice-skates, angled into the ice to prevent drift. At the front of the boat (usually) is a blade that can be manoeuvred for the purpose of sterring. Ice boats are sail-powered and are generally one-person or two-person vehicles. They are aerodynamically very efficient, and the friction on the ice is minimal, so they can accelerate to speeds much higher than the ambient wind speed. Speeds of 60 miles per hour (96 km per hour) are not uncommon, and much higher speeds have been recorded, up to and beyond 150 miles per hour (240kph). Hybrid ice boats that can hop off ice into open water and back again also exist.

Ice boating is usually undertaken on lakes and rivers in northern latitudes where low temperatures guarantee a solid freeze, but where snowfall does not come too early: a lumpy covering of snow makes ice boating impossible. So the premier spots for 'hard water sailing' (as *aficionados* call it) tend to be northern America, Canada and Scandinavia, though ice boating is also encountered in more southerly locations such as Hungary's Lake Balaton.

It's rather a specialized sport, but if you live near the right sort of 'hard water' and can afford to hire the equipment, add it to your winter list.

70.

MAKE A SNOFA

A snofa is a snow sofa: a sofa made out of snow you can sit on. Every front garden should have one.

First of all, get a good mound of snow together. Your starting mound should be a rough rectangular block, a bit bigger than the finished sofa will be. Make sure the block is as compacted as possible: stamp it down hard while you are building it. Tamp it down with planks if possible. For optimum compaction, wettish snow, rather than powdery snow, is best.

Now think about your design. What sort of arms do you want? Will they be rounded or square? Will the arms project slightly at the side, requiring an undercut? How much will the back slope? Will there be a recess at the base to suggest legs? Look at pictures of sofas or examine your own living-room sofa to see where some of the opportunities lie.

Now begin the carving process. Start with a spade

or shovel to rough out the shape, then use a fairly thin sharp tool with a flat blade – a paint scraper is perfect – to work on the finer details, such as the cushion divisions and the arm design. Stand back often and squint at it to check for symmetry.

When the snofa is finished to your satisfaction, mist it with water. This will form an icy layer and will make it strong enough to sit down on. You can mist using a houseplant mister or a hose on a fine spray setting. Wait for each misted layer to freeze, then apply another, like successive coats of varnish.

Now build an igloo around it (see §91).

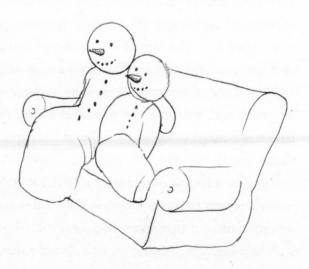

71.

RUN EVEREST

Most of the activities in this book are more or less practical: anyone can make their own linocut Christmas cards, brew mulled wine, go ice skating or have a snowball fight.

Running Everest, one might think, is somewhat different. But in fact it's eminently do-able. The runners do not race *to* the top; they start *at* the top – or rather half-way up, at Gorak Shep, 17,000 feet (5184m) up, near the Nepalese Everest Base Camp. They then run the standard marathon length of 26.2 miles (42 km), finishing much lower down, at Namche Bazaar, a Sherpa town, at 11,300 feet (3446m). So it's all downhill!

There are a couple of upward stretches, as well as the potential hazards of tripping over yaks and negotiating rope-bridges, but that's to be expected. The organizers do additionally recommend that you have experience of rough-terrain high-altitude running, and have a couple of off-road marathons under your belt.

It seems to be tempting fate to actually hold it in winter (it's in November or December) but apparently winter on Everest is not as bad as it sounds.

So altogether this is one of the more practical ideas in this book. And the Everest Marathon is a non-profit-making activity. All sponsorship money goes to charities benefiting Nepalese communities.

72.

INAUGURATE A CHRISTMAS SPORT

Christmas can be a passive time: eat, watch TV, lapse into a coma. Shorn of its religious and traditional associations and activities (carol singing, party games, puppet shows) it can breed a species of depression – Yule Torpor, one might call it.

One way to make things more active and beat Yule Torpor is to inaugurate a Christmas sport.

Older readers might remember a time when Christmas football matches or running races were popular. My suggestion to those eager to resurrect a Christmas sport, is tug-of-war.

When Baron Pierre de Coubertin resurrected the idea of an Olympic Games modelled on the Panhellenic Games of Ancient Greece, tug-of-war had an honoured place. In 1920, sadly, it was shelved as an Olympic sport, but has made a comeback as a winter sport. At root a contest of brute force, it nevertheless has a lengthy rule book and an element of strategy. Among its chief difficulties is that it is one of the few sports where 'foul language' is specifically forbidden.

Try it at Christmas with the family, friends and neighbours. Post flyers through doors if necessary. Buy a piece of proper tug of war rope (don't use a washing line: it will break!) Allot teams. Clear the streets with marshals wearing fluorescent jackets.

73.

MAKE YOUR OWN CHRISTMAS COSAQUES

Simon Callow in his book *Dickens's Christmas* tells us that the Christmas cracker was originally called a 'Cosaque', after the fierce cavalry of the Tsar. The term 'cracker' was later substituted, and the first crackers contained love messages ('Be Mine', 'Meet me in the Scullery', etc.)

To reproduce some of the flavour of the Victorian Christmas, you can make your own Cosaques. Start with a sheet of good-quality wrapping paper, about 12in (30cm) long and 10in (20cm) wide. Lay it out flat and make two perforations running up the shorter side, about 3in (8cm) from each edge: these allow the Cosaque to break when pulled. You can make perforations by lightly scoring the paper with a craft knife, or by using a perforation wheel (cheap at craft shops). Now lay onto the paper three cardboard tubes from a kitchen roll or loo roll, the middle one larger than the outlying two. Add a cracker snap, glued to the top (long length) of the paper at both ends: cracker snaps, which supply the bang, can be bought very cheaply by the dozen. Now roll the paper up along the longer axis and tie a ribbon between the first two cardboard rolls to seal it. Fill up the Cosaque with gifts and treats – don't forget the love messages – then seal the other end. Decorate with glitter, holly, tinsel or anything that looks good.

Since you're making your own, you might like to put something really worthwhile inside: real Swiss chocolate, perhaps, or lottery tickets. Add a paper hat (see the next section) and you're all set.

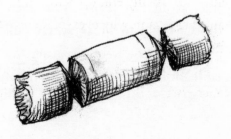

74.

MAKE CHRISTMAS HATS

A Christmas dinner is not complete without paper hats, which do an excellent job of making everyone appear vaguely ridiculous.

To make your own, use coloured tissue paper (this scrunches up nicely to fit inside your Christmas Cosaques; see above). Get a piece about 26 inches (66cm) long and about seven inches (18cm) high. Fold it and glue it so it forms a circle: check it on your head first to make sure it fits. (You're going to be making them for a variety of head sizes, so let's assume your head is typical; otherwise find a typical head. Because Christmas hats are by their very nature 'one size fits all', they usually end up being slightly too big, which is another reason why everyone ends up looking vaguely ridiculous).

Next, fold up your circle of tissue paper laterally – once, twice, three times – so it forms a piece about three inches wide. Then take a sharp pair of scissors or a craft knife and cut the points of the crown on the top edge. Just a few points will do: when you unfold the tissue paper the points will appear all the way around the rim.

Finally use the craft knife or scissors to cut other patterns in the paper: a couple of stars or triangles perhaps. When it's unfolded this will make a rather beautiful lacy effect.

To decorate, use glitter: apply glue first, in whichever patterns you have in mind, then shake the glitter on top and wait for it to dry.

75.

MAKE AN ADVENT CALENDAR

Anticipation is the greater part of pleasure, and for this reason Advent calendars are among the most delightful of Christmas traditions.

Advent is the season that starts at the beginning of December and extends to the 25th: the official start varies, falling between the 27th of November and the 3rd of December, but most advent calendars ignore the liturgical timing and start plumb on the 1st, making 25 days in all.

If you want to make your own, there are various different designs, some using little boxes, others using cloth pockets, and so on: the simplest is probably the flat upright design made of card. To try this, first find a sturdy base, such as a piece of thick cardboard. Then get a picture of the same size to lay over it. You can draw your own, or maybe use a print of a Christmas scene. Now create a gap between them. Build a tiny wall about a quarter of an inch (half a centimetre) high around the perimeter of the base, using some more cardboard. Glue it in place. Now make some supporting struts of the same height on the main body of the base. When you pop the cover on, it will be supported.

Cut windows in the cover with a craft knife. You need to do this so the window-lines are scored, but not completely cut through (which takes practice, so experiment first). Cut three sides for each window and leave the top uncut as a hinge. Underneath the windows put whatever you like: perhaps pound coins and pennies, alternating randomly, so the children never know which they're going to get. Stick them in place so they don't rattle around.

You can also put in little pictures or wise sayings, but, believe me, these are not as popular.

76.

HEAR HANDEL'S MESSIAH

The Messiah is George Frideric Handel's best-known work, and your best opportunity to hear it is around Christmas time. The best-known bit of this best-known work is the 'Hallelujah chorus', which is often performed on its own, though in context it's the climax to Part II of the Messiah, about two-thirds of the way through. The real climax is the magnificent and thunderous 'Amen' at the end of the final part, which one commentator wrote in 1760 'eclipses even that vast effort of genius, the Hallelujah chorus'.

Originally the Messiah was written for only a small chorus and small orchestra, but the tradition has been to stage it with ever-larger bodies of singers and players, giving it an almost apocalyptic feel (it was written to announce the coming of the Messiah, after all, and there isn't really a bigger subject). George Bernard Shaw found this megalomania rather tiresome.

'Why,' he wrote, 'instead of wasting huge sums on the multitudinous dullness of a Handel Festival, does not somebody set up a thoroughly rehearsed and exhaustively studied performance of the Messiah in St James' Hall with a chorus of twenty capable artists? Most of us would be glad to hear the work seriously performed once before we die.'

77.

DRIVE IN THE DESERT

In 1978 a young man called Thierry Sabine realized his dream by inaugurating the first Paris-Dakar rally. This was a race by dune buggy from Paris through Spain to the deserts of North Africa, finishing broken in mind and body on the banks of the Pink Lake in Dakar, Senegal. In between were the gruelling ergs (shifting dunes) of Mauritania, the scorching sands of the Sahel, and the maze-like tracks of the Senegalese savannah – though some drivers reported that the worst parts were the *autopistas* of southern Spain.

Since then, the Paris-Dakar rally has been held every year in January, and has become one of the most televised rally events in the world. Strangely enough, it doesn't start in Paris any more. And it doesn't go to Dakar. In 2008, after terrorist incidents in North Africa, the entire race was re-routed to South America, where it has remained. The race currently runs from Lima to Santiago. In a magnificent denial of reality, it's still called 'the Dakar', and the trophy depicts a person wearing a Berber head-dress.

So, if you are inclined this January, go and cheer on the racers, or participate yourself in any of the four classes: motorbike, quad bike, car and truck. Or watch it on TV.

Equipment needed: water, GPS system, distress beacon, and headset playing a loop of the theme tune to 'Wacky Races'.

78.

RUN UP A BUILDING

Running in winter gives a feeling of virtue. Everyone else is bundling along morosely in padded jackets and inch-thick socks, and you are bare-legged, bare-armed, exhaling like a dragon, and feeling great.

There are unfortunately some serious disadvantages. Pavements can be slushy and slippery, and the evenings and mornings are dark. And it's hard to motivate yourself to get out there in the freezing weather even if you know you're going to love it once you warm up.

With this in mind, why not try tower running? It's the ideal winter sport. Essentially it's running up a high building, usually by using the internal staircases. The first tower run, inaugurated in 1978, was the Empire State Run-Up, which is still held every year in February, and the record for its 86 floors and 1,576 steps is 9 minutes 33 seconds, set by Paul Crake in 2003. The run is for charity, and the competitors are a mix of professional and amateur marathon, cross-country and mountain runners, as well as kids, the elderly and the publicity-hungry.

You don't need to buy a plane ticket to New York. There are now run-ups on all continents. In Britain there is the 'Vertical Rush' at Tower 42, and the Gherkin Challenge at... the Gherkin. There are also tower runs at Taipei 101 in Taiwan, the Eureka Tower in Melbourne, the Kuala Lumpur Tower in Malaysia and many other places.

The main danger is possibly that when you get to the top you'll forget what you've gone up for.

79.

OBSERVE THE WINTER SOLSTICE

This is the day, December 21st or 22nd, when the day is shortest and the night longest. The sun rises painfully only just above the horizon, only to creep back shortly afterwards as if it had made a mistake. And in northern latitudes the misery is only just beginning. The three or four months that follow the winter solstice are the hardest to endure. No crops grow. Temperatures decline. Whatever humans eat must have been stored up well in advance. In these hungry months, people in former times died of famine and cold.

Paradoxically, though, the winter solstice has always been a time of celebration. Whatever happens after the solstice is all in the right direction: the days lengthen, the nights shorten and the sun climbs, even if it takes a long time to warm our bones. Religions that worship dying and rising gods (such as Christianity) do so at or near the solstice. It was a convenient occasion for feasting. Fermented liquors from the harvests of autumn were newly available. Animals that could not be fed during the lean times were slaughtered, providing an abundance of red meat. The winter solstice was an 'eat, drink and be merry, for tomorrow...' sort of festival.

Almost every culture (except equatorial ones) marks the solstice in some way, leading to a clustering of festivals in late December. One of the most charming is St Lucy's Day in Scandinavia, on which girls dress in white, carry candles and sweets, and visit the sick and elderly. *Lusekatter* (Lucy cat) buns are eaten (probably an echo of the goddess Freya, whose chariot was drawn by cats), washed down the mulled wine known as *gløgg*.

80.

BURN THE CLOCKS

'Burning the clocks' is a festival held every year in Brighton on the winter solstice, so if you're not inclined to observe the date by slaughtering an ox, you can head to the south coast and do something more vegetarian. It attracts more than 2,000 marchers and 20,000 spectators annually, making it one of Britain's biggest public celebrations. Despite that, it's comparatively recent. It started in 1994 as a community initiative and has increased in popularity ever since.

Replicas of clocks made out of wicker and paper, lit up inside like lanterns, are carried to Brighton beach, and ceremonially burned amid a spectacular fire and fireworks show. Originally, replicas of the clock towers in Brighton were used (a rebellion against the civic authorities?), though in subsequent years there have been other themes, such as 'The Death of Time' (drawing on 'Day of the Dead' motifs), 'The Garden of Time', and 'Drowned Time'. The idea is to mark the end of the solar year, saying goodbye to the old sun and welcoming the new: perhaps its symbolism also lies in jettisoning the errors of the past or in finding a liberation from the time-constraints of day-to-day living. Local groups such as Woodcraft make clock-lanterns for the parades, and families can buy a lantern pack to make themselves. Poorer areas of the town are provided with free lantern-making workshops.

Because it's held so close to Christmas, 'Burning the Clocks' is also something of a rival to the dominant festival of the month; and because the only gifts ever given are immediately burned, perhaps its an antidote to the over-commercialization of the season.

81.

TURN THE TABLES

A list of solstice festivals could extend to 102 and beyond. One that must be mentioned – the grandparent of them all, considering that it originated in the Latin culture that dominated Europe for centuries – is Saturnalia, the Roman festival of dissipation celebrated annually around the time of the lowest declination of the sun.

Saturn was the deity who presided over the golden age at the infancy of mankind. Under his rule, human beings lived in peace and plenty, with no man being the master of any other; Saturnalia, the festival of Saturn, was an attempt to re-create this golden age with gift-giving, feasting and family celebrations, but also with a tradition of role reversals. According to Roman sources, slaves were served a banquet, sometimes by their masters, and free speech was permitted. The Roman writer Horace in his *Satires* has a slave speak thus to his master at Saturnalia: 'Why do you willfully call me to account, as if you were the better man; and, with specious phrases, disguise your own vice? What, if you are found out to be a greater fool than me, who was purchased for five hundred drachmas?' A King of Saturnalia was also elected, whose commands had to be followed, however absurd: 'Tie a swan to his back and throw him from the temple roof' being an extreme recorded example. Later European traditions concerning the 'Lord of Misrule' were very probably influenced by the King of Saturnalia.

As the success of 'Burning the Clocks' (see above, §80) shows, new festivals to replace or complement Christmas can be hugely popular; perhaps Saturnalia, with its tearing-up of the rule book and delight in shock and role-reversal, is just what we need.

82.

START AN ALLOTMENT

Many people start an allotment in spring, when it's time to plant things. This makes a lot of sense, since most crops – especially root crops such as potatoes or beetroot, or salad crops and brassicas – shouldn't be put in the ground until after the last frosts.

However, there is also a powerful rationale for starting earlier, as far back as December. Why? Because allotments are not just about planting. If you inherit an allotment it could be (and often will be) in a bit of a state, full of old tyres and bits of wood. There may be rotting greenhouses or sheds on it that you want to clear away or replace. And you are going to need to undertake some serious preparations in terms of the soil itself. Weeding is a huge job on an untended or neglected allotment. You'll have to dig the ground and create beds. You'll need to fertilize and condition. It's no good starting in spring and then finding out you've taken on a massive plot that you can't control.

And actually there's a lot you can plant in the winter months too. Garlic can be planted in December. Japanese onions likewise. Broad beans can go in in February. And early potatoes can go in at the beginning of March (which is technically spring, but most of the time it still feels like winter).

In winter there won't be the light in the evenings and mornings, which is a small problem, but winter weekends are an absolutely ideal time to work up a sweat. When spring comes everything will be shipshape and you'll be ready to get planting.

83.

HAVE A SNOWBALL FIGHT

A snowball fight always teeters on the edge of aggression, but, ideally, never steps over it. Acts of mercy must leaven acts of war.

Work with the personnel you have. If you have a group, form teams. If you are one dad against three children, the common practice is for them to gang up on you and for you to lose. There may be rules; there may not be. Rules help keep it good-natured and avoid tears. 'No throwing at faces' is one good rule: 'no snow down the neck' is another. 'No throwing when a player is on a home base' allows for recovery time. 'No ice' and 'no rocks' are also sensible. For every rule there will be a rat, but rats are omnipresent in every walk of life.

For serious snowball fighting, try constructing a snow-forts in opposing territories. Pack the snow down hard and hunker behind. With a fort as your protection you can build up your stock of ammo.

Players can take turns to be armament-makers and bombardiers. The winner is the team that destroys the opposing fort and forces the other team into retreat.

Or try starting the biggest ever snowball fight in your area. Let people know about it on social networks. Invite the local press.

One tip: make sure you have plenty of warm, waterproof clothing and good waterproof gloves. Woollen gloves are not ideal as they quickly become sodden.

84.

PLAY SNOWBALL 'CAPTURE THE FLAG'

Snowball fighting can actually be a serious competitive sport, believe it or not. It has various titles, including 'snowball CTF' (snowball Capture the Flag) and '*yukigassen*', and is played in nations like Finland, Norway and Japan, where White Christmases are virtually guaranteed.

In snowball CTF, two teams compete to capture a flag or other object (perhaps a large glowstick or a ball) in one of two opposing territories. Teams are of equal numbers, usually around seven apiece. Teams start off on their home sides and must try to infiltrate each other's sides without being 'tagged' (in this case, hit with a snowball). Tagged players can be put in jail, where they languish until a fellow teammember springs them by touching them. Sometimes a single touch can release all the jailed members; in other versions, they can only be released one at a time. Once in the opposing side, each team must try to steal the flag and run with it back to their territory. Coordinated snowball attacks on the defenders of the flag create diversions so that offensive players can sneak in and grab the prize without being tagged.

In professional circles, players wear helmets with face-screens, and work with a limited number of pre-made snowballs formed to regulation shape and size.

This seems to take all the fun out of it, but perhaps that's just me.

85.

SEE IN THE CHINESE NEW YEAR

The Chinese New Year is a festival of extraordinary antiquity. Chinese years are numbered from the time of the Yellow Emperor Huangdi in the 3rd millennium BC (Huangdi was a semi-legendary figure who invented the bow sling, the zither, astronomy and the Chinese calendar itself, which shows that you have to be in it to win it). The next Chinese New Year will be numbered somewhere in the 4000s, which knocks most other calendars into a cocked hat.

As most people know, each Chinese New Year is associated with one of twelve animals. If you were born in a certain year, aspects of that animal's personality accrue to you. Nice, perhaps, if you are a tiger or possibly a horse, but requiring a certain humility if you are a sheep or a rat.

Starting in late January to mid-February, the Chinese New Year is celebrated over fifteen days and is a time for special family meals, visiting relatives, letting off fireworks, participating in lion dances, and decorating homes with red lanterns. Since there are Chinese New Year celebrations all around the world, it's easy to join in!

The lanterns, dancing and fireworks are all related to the myth of the Nian. The Nian was a fearsome monster that attacked villages at the New Year, but one day a fearless child wearing red managed to check its ravages. The villagers realized that the Nian was scared of red! The lion dancing, the red decorations and the loud noises are all to scare the Nian – 4,000 years down the line.

86.

TAKE A WINTER HIKE

The hiking season is summer. Well, that's what most people think. But with a few precautions, winter is a superb time to get out and enjoy the countryside. Snow-covered mountains, trees filigreed with frost, black crows against the bare winter landscape, ice-skaters on a pond seen from high on a hill... these are some of the delights of winter walking.

So, first check the weather forecast. Don't go if it's snowing or raining, since this will get you down and leach much of the joy from the experience. Second, get some good walking clothes. The secret is to dress in layers: underneath, something in a man-made fibre, since cotton gets wet quickly from sweat and doesn't dry out; in the middle, a padded insulation layer, though not too thick, since you don't want your movements to be restricted; and on top, your weather protection system, a waterproof layer. For the hands, gloves; for the head, a hat (with earflaps that can be lowered if necessary, though you wouldn't want to miss out on the sounds of the winter landscape – crunch of snow, caw of bird, bleat of lamb) and for the feet, waterproofed boots with good traction and at least two pairs of socks. As already pointed out, winter is really all about socks.

Take maps, a small medical kit and a phone (keep the phone close to your body where it's warm, because batteries drain more quickly in colder weather).

Perhaps the best of it is that you'll be substantially on your own. Winter landscapes are best appreciated in silence and solitude. In winter, the snow-covered world is miraculously renewed, and you can be the first to discover it.

87.

CELEBRATE HANNUKAH

Hannukah is an eight-day Jewish celebration of thanksgiving. It's a moveable feast celebrated every year, and can start any time from late November to late December, so it usually coincides with the Christmas period.

Hannukah's origins are in the second century BCE, during the period when the Jews were under the domination of the Seleucid (Syrian-Greek) kings. In 165 BCE a Jewish revolt was successful in throwing off the Seleucid yoke and recapturing the temple, which was in need of a good clean. The story goes that oil was needed to light the menorahs (the multi-branched candlesticks) in the temple, but there was only enough to burn for one day. However, this one-day supply miraculously lasted for eight days, and an eight-day festival was instituted to commemorate the fact.

Hannukah is usually a private celebration held in the home, with lots of traditional games and customs, such as the spinning of tradonal tops called *dreidels*, and the giving of small money presents to children. Menorahs with nine branches (one extra for giving light to see by) are placed in windows, and larger versions are sometimes lit in public places. Hannukah is also celebrated every year with a party in the White House (not yet, as far as I am aware, in Downing Street). One tradition that non-Jews can happily share in is the food: *latkes* (potato pancakes), *sufganiyot* (doughnuts flavoured with jam but also many other fillings) and cheese-flavoured products (such as cheese *blintzes* and cheesecake).

88.

WASSAIL AN ORCHARD

If you want to make sure the apple crop is magnificent come September, the way to do it is to sing to the trees in January.

Wassailing is an ancient English custom observed in the cider-growing counties of the south-west. It takes place at the lowest point of the year, in January, and it's not always easy to force oneself to stand in a denuded orchard in sub-zero temperatures, doing things that are faintly silly. A goodly intake of cider helps, though.

The first stage of wassailing is to process *en masse* to the tree and offer its roots some of last year's cider. If you have a Wassail King or Queen to do the offering, so much the better. You can also hang a slice of ham in the branches of the oldest tree. Then you sing wassailing songs. These will vary from region to region, but might include verses such as:

> *Old apple tree we wassail thee*
> *And hoping thou will bear*
> *Hat fulls, cap fulls, three bushel bag fulls*
> *And all of them sound and fair.*

Then you should make as much noise as you can. This is very definitely a big part of the ceremony. Bang pots and pans; scream; or let off guns. The idea is to terrify the spirits who might wish to possess the trees and stunt their growth.

Wassailing might seem like a defunct custom but it's very much alive in the 'cider triangle'. When the cider could be in peril, any measures, however ridiculous, are fully justified.

89.

WATCH A GOAT-BURNING

In Scandinavia there is a custom of making goats out of straw for Christmas. Nowadays they are most commonly seen as small Christmas decorations. However, in some parts of Scandinavia, enormous straw goats, as high as four-storey buildings, are erected in the centres of towns.

This would probably be little known in the rest of the world, if the goats were not subject to repeated arson attacks.

The first goat erected was the brainchild of an advertising copywriter, Stig Gavlen, in the town of Gavle in Sweden in 1966. On New Year's Eve that year it was torched by vandals, and, being made of straw, burned rapidly to the ground. In following years the goat was re-erected, but again attacked by vandals with matches, petrol and flaming arrows. In one year it was run over by a car and on other occasions kicked to pieces or thrown in the river. The attacks spread across Sweden, with copycat (copygoat?) attacks in several other towns. The goats seemed to inspire animosity. 'Burn the goat!' was the cry that rang out across Sweden.

However, in a strange side-effect, the war between the towns' burghers and the vandals led to an increase of tourism in goat-erecting areas. Some even wondered whether the authorities were tacitly allowing the goats to be torched. This was, and is, strongly denied. The goats cost a great deal to put up, and further sums of money are spent every year on flame-retardant chemicals, fencing and security guards.

They seem to do little good.

90.

MAKE A SNOW GLOBE

Snow globes are the little hemispheres that simulate snowing when you turn them upside down. These charming micro-worlds are oddly absorbing.

To make one, first of all get a small jar of clear glass. A baby-food jar is fine. Remove the label and take off the lid. Paint the lid with enamel paint so as to obliterate the name of the manufacturer. (There is no room for commercialization at Christmas.)

Now take the lid and arrange your scene on its underside. It might be a nativity with Jesus and some farm animals; it might be a snowman; or it might be something totally unexpected, like a cactus and a bleached skull. Glue everything down firmly with water-resistant glue.

Fill up the jar with water and add some glitter. Add a teaspoon of glycerine to the water: this thickens it and stops the snowstorm blowing itself out too quickly.

Glycerine can be bought at chemists. Alternatively you can use baby oil instead of water.

Screw the lid on tight. If you're sure you won't ever want to get it off again to change the scene, seal the inside of the lid first with glue.

Make a dozen, line them up, and practice getting them all to snow at the same time.

91.

BUILD AN IGLOO

Or how about a different type of snow globe, one you can live inside? Building an igloo is not difficult. You really only need one thing: lots of snow. A 12-inch (30 cm) snowfall is the minimum requirement, preferably with good compaction.

Carve your blocks out of the ground using a saw or sharp stick. If you've got less snow, or your snow is very powdery, you can still create blocks by using a mould: shovel the snow into the mould and tamp it down before turning it out. A washing-up bowl, recycling bin or large ice-cream tub will serve.

Form a circular base to start with, laying out the blocks and plugging the triangular gaps between blocks with handfuls of snow. Don't bother leaving a space for an entrance. That comes later. Pile on the second level of blocks, placing them a little further in, then more levels, until you approach the apex. It will be easier if you have two people working, one inside and one outside. At the apex, fit blocks of various sizes to form the cap. Once the cap is in place, the distribution of forces will make your igloo a very stable structure.

Now hack out a door. Dig down a little so the entryway is as far below the floor as possible, to prevent loss of heat. A properly constructed igloo with a few bodies snuggled inside will attain a temperature well above freezing. Cut grooves into the ceiling to channel any drips of melt down to the sides. Also make a small ventilation hole somewhere near the top. Add a torch and some walrus blubber.

92.

MAKE A SNOW CAVE

There's a simpler way of doing the same thing. Make a snow cave. A snow cave is just like an igloo, but it's formed by piling up a solid dome of snow, then excavating the space inside.

Start by gathering a few friends and building up a mound of snow until it's around person-height. Compact it as much as possible.

When you've got your dome, tunnel into it from below, so that the shaft goes slightly upwards. This is so the final interior space has an entryway lower than the floor, preventing heat loss. While you are tunnelling and excavating, always have friends on standby on the outside. If the snow collapses on top of you, you may not be able to get out alone.

While you're inside digging, you won't be sure how far to go and may break through to the fresh air. An easy way to avoid this is to push some short sticks through from the outside wall, so that whenever you hit a stick, you know to stop digging. You'll also be able to create thinner walls this way, so if there's a collapse, it won't be too heavy.

Level out the floor and get in with some warm clothing and some hot chocolate. As with the igloo, make grooves in the ceiling to channel drips, and build in a ventilation hole or two. Don't build a fire, since you'll breathe in the smoke – and it could cause collapse.

Don't do this alone!

93.

MAKE A SURVIVALIST'S SNOW TRENCH

For an even simpler snow shelter, of truly budget proportions, try a snow trench. This is not going to be the most comfortable snow accommodation in the world, but it's quick to make – quicker than either an igloo or a snow cave – and if you're alone and lost in a freezing wilderness, it could come in very handy.

As the name suggests, a snow trench is just a person-shaped dugout in the snow. You need a heavy snow cover to make one, ideally around two to three feet (60–90cm). Cut into the snow with a saw or blade if you have one, or a sharp stick if you don't. Lever out the blocks and stack them up: you'll need them later. Widen out the hole until you can get in it and lie down, but don't make it too wide or long or you'll lose too much body heat when you take up residence.

Bevelling the hole, so that the base is wider than the top, also helps reduce heat loss.

Now, get the blocks you've excavated and position them on top of the trench in an A-frame design, creating a sort of gabled roof. Leave some room at one end, then get in and position the last two blocks from the inside. Make sure you've got an air-hole to avoid carbon dioxide build-up. Now get your sleeping bag and lie down there in the snug. Actually you won't be all that snug, and there won't be any room to toast marshmallows, but you'll be out of the wind and at a temperature marginally above freezing.

94.

TOSS A TUNA

Tuna Tossing is the highlight of the Tunarama Festival held at Port Lincoln, South Australia, every year on Australia Day weekend, around the 26th January. It involves tossing a dead tuna the maximum distance possible. The sport originates from the local fishing industry, in which, in former times, tuna were thrown from the fishing boats to waiting lorries. In the Tuna Toss, competitors stand in a small circle similar to a hammer-throwing circle, and fling the tuna by means of a rope handle. Given a whirling start, the results can be pretty spectacular: at least the cheering crowds on the foreshore seem to think so.

The fish for the event weigh in at around 20lbs (9kg) each for both the men's and the women's events, but in 2007 a momentous decision was taken: fake rubberised tuna were substituted for the real fish, due to ecological concerns. Real tuna are only used for the finals, though they remain the fish of choice for all serious practitioners.

'The world's greatest tosser' is ex-Olympic hammer-thrower Sean Carlin, whose world record, set in 1998, still stands: 122.14 feet (37.23 m).

Of course, you might not be in South Australia this winter, but if you need a good excuse to escape to the southern hemisphere in January, this is surely it.

95.

FRY ICE-CREAM

Fried ice-cream is a reality (as Funkadelic sang in the 1970s). For those who haven't tried it, here's a recipe.

Get six to eight of scoops of ice-cream and freeze them individually on a baking sheet. After an hour or two, remove them from the freezer and coat them with beaten egg-whites. Roll the eggy ice-cream in a coating of your choice: crushed cornflakes are good, but you can also choose crushed nuts, crushed biscuits or cake mixture. Return to the freezer and allow them to solidify for at least another three hours. After this, fire up a saucepan or deep-frying pan full of oil. Wait until the oil is at chip-frying temperature (test it by putting a few cornflakes in) and then gently lower the balls, a couple at a time, into the oil. They will splatter and fizz but as long as the ice-cream is really cold and well-coated with crumbs, they will fry rather like pieces of chicken or scotch eggs. Keep the balls in the oil for thirty seconds or so until golden brown. Remove and place on some kitchen towels. Serve immediately, drizzled with chocolate sauce, whipped cream, chopped nuts, maraschino cherries or all four.

Alternatively you can substitute pancake batter for the egg. Make up a thickish batter so that it coats the frozen balls well, and then roll them in crushed cereal, crumbs, nuts etc., as before. This gives a thicker coating and protects the ice-cream more effectively while frying.

Crispy and hot without, cold and creamy within – a minor winter miracle.

96.

RACE WITH A FRYING PAN

Another frying-pan-related activity is the Pancake Race at Olney in Buckinghamshire. It's held every year on Shrove Tuesday, the Tuesday before Lent, making it Buckinghamshire's answer to *Mardi Gras*.

The race dates from 1445. Tradition has it that the first racer was a woman who was late for the shriving service (held for the forgiveness of sins), and, running frantically from her house to the church, forgot that she was still carrying her frying pan.

Nowadays the race is open to women over 18 years old who have lived in the village for at least three months prior to the race. Each contestant must wear the traditional uniform of the housewife, an apron and a headscarf, and must be carrying a frying pan. The distance is 415 yards, from the market to the parish church, and each contestant must toss her pancake at least once at the beginning of the race and once at the end. There are various prizes, and winners get a kiss from the verger. The record time for the course is 56 seconds (set by Devon Byrne in 2013), though the kissing may last longer.

Places in the race are currently limited to 25, so competition is fierce. If you can't join in, you can spectate. Or start you own winter race tradition!

97.

MAKE SNOW RABBITS OR OTHER SNOW ANIMALS

Snow rabbits are easy. Just get a couple of handfuls of snow and pat them into something about the same size and shape as a rugby ball. At one end, above the nose (you need a bit of imagination to see a nose at this point) add two berries – perhaps holly berries – to serve as eyes. Then, above them and spaced wider apart, add two leaves of an evergreen shrub (camellia, laurel, holly) to serve as ears. That's it. Make one or a hundred: dot them around the garden or put them on walls or gateposts. Or take them inside and watch them plaintively melt. One rabbit per day to keep you company.

Or you can make other snow-creatures. Try a snow cat. For a sitting snow cat, form a large ball of snow, then shape the cat's rump and back legs so it looks like it's sitting with its legs folded underneath it. Add a tail curling around it on the ground. In front, fashion two supporting legs: these can be added as columns of snow or shaped out of the existing snow. Make a separate ball for the head and pop it on top. Spend some time getting the face-shape and ears right. You can use berries or buttons or coal for the eyes, or anything else that comes to hand, though the cold white minimalism of the snow may be preferable.

98.

CELEBRATE KWANZAA

Kwanzaa is another winter festival, this time one coming hard on the heels of Christmas. It starts on Boxing Day, 26th December, and runs until the 1st January.

Kwanzaa originated in the USA in the context of the Black Liberation movement of the 60s. Its founder, Maulana Karenga, created it as the first specifically African-American-orientated holiday: since then it has spread to countries such as Canada and France, and is now a more general celebration of Pan-African culture and identity. The name Kwanzaa comes from the Swahili for 'first fruits' (*matunda ya kwanza*).

Kwanzaa is not a religious festival but a cultural one, so people of all religions can take part. All races are included, so if you are not of African heritage there is nothing stopping you from meditating on Black history and identity.

Coming so near Christmas, it means that participants can celebrate Christmas if they wish, and then, after swallowing some aspirin, transition seamlessly into Kwanzaa.

The celebration itself focuses on seven communitarian African values, the Nguzo Saba. These are (in Swahili): *Umoja* (unity), *Kujichagulia* (self-determination), *Ujima* (collective work and responsibility), *Ujamaa* (cooperative economics), *Nia* (purpose), *Kuumba* (creativity), and *Imani* (faith). The Kwanzaa greeting is: '*Habari gani?*' and the answer differs according to the day, so on the first day of Kwanzaa the response is '*Umoja*', on the second day, '*Kujichagulia*', and so on.

99.

TOAST MARSHMALLOWS OVER AN OPEN FIRE

Perhaps you're having a winter beach party, and are gathered around the fire pit listening to the waves roar onto the shore. Or you're huddled around a campfire in the woods, wondering about bears. Or you're at home in front of the grate, watching the coals die down and nursing a glass of sherry. What is needed to make the experience complete? Marshmallows, naturally.

Very few things in nature undergo the transmutation that a toasted marshmallow does. Raw marshmallows are only vaguely interesting lumps of spongy stuff. A perfectly toasted marshmallow is a treat fit for the gods, at once gooey, crispy, sweet and delicious.

The definition of 'perfectly toasted' is open to interpretation, of course. Some elect to have them golden brown all over and cooked all the way through, with perhaps only the tiniest central portion still untouched by the heat so the stick has something to hold onto. This is best achieved by holding the marshmallow on a long stick next to embers rather than naked flames, and turning regularly. Others prefer briefly to incinerate the marshmallow in the flames and pop it in their mouths *in flagrante*. Yet others have deeper, darker desires: they inline towards marshmallows pre-filled with jam or chocolate, giving an even greater sensual experience of sugar and goo.

Or for those who wish to send their blood sugar levels rocketing to the point where they have an out-of-body experience, there are 's'mores'. These are toasted marshmallows combined with chocolate between two biscuits and eaten like a sandwich.

100.

PLAY ELEPHANT POLO

Also known as: elepolo

When: December

Equipment: Two metre polo stick; elephant

Prize: Silver plated *quaiches* (drinking bowls/cups) sponsored by Chivas Regal

Notable recent winner: The Duke of Argyll

Elephant polo is played in many countries throughout south-east Asia, including Nepal, India, Sri Lanka and Thailand. The World Championships are in December in Kathmandu, making it the quintessential winter sport. Although it's expensive, players from anywhere and everywhere turn up in Nepal to get on ele-back, including teams from Scotland, England and Switzerland.

Each game in elephant polo consists of two 10-minute *chukkas* using two-metre mallets but a regulation polo ball. Each elephant carries a *mahout*, or driver, plus a player with a mallet. The pitch is smaller than a regulation polo pitch, and rules are similar to pony polo, with a few exceptions: an elephant lying in front of the goal mouth constitutes a foul. Each team must have an elephant in each half at all times. Elephants are not permitted to pick up the ball in their trunks.

Elephant welfare is a priority. Elephants tire quickly, and are not allowed to play in any two consecutive *chukkas*. Ele-snacks are on hand, consisting of sugar cane or rice balls fortified with molasses and rock salt.

Originally soccer balls were used, but the elephants enjoyed popping them.

101.

PLANT A LIVING WILLOW FENCE

'Good fences make good neighbours.'
- 17th century proverb

Various species of plants can be used to make fences (or 'fedges' – a combination of fence and hedge), but willow has some significant advantages. It's very hardy and easy to plant, grows very rapidly, and is supple, so it can be bent into different forms.

So, if you agree that good fences make good neighbours, why not try it in your back garden? First of all you need to buy some willow rods or 'setts'. These are just willow twigs cut to the right length for planting. Starting in December though to March, plant them about a foot (30 cm) deep in the ground, spaced about a foot apart. Don't plant them too near building foundations or drainage pipes: willow roots are very invasive and may cause damage. Willows enjoy wet soil (which is why they grow near river-banks) so if your soil is very dry, regular watering is important.

In the spring, your willow will begin to sprout: leave it to grow as it wishes, and only prune after the leaves have dropped in autumn. You can then prune to the desired height of the hedge, or cut the rods off low (known as 'coppicing') to create a thicker, sturdier hedge.

Willow can also be used for other structures. In fact, your imagination is the only limit. You can make living willow arches, domes, igloos, tunnels, arbours and grottoes. You can even make a living willow bench or sculpture. And because it's alive, it will never rot or decay; on the contrary, it will get thicker and stronger with every year.

102.

REMEMBER THAT WINTER ENDS

Winter doesn't last forever. Spring is around the corner. Yes, the days will get longer, lambs will be born, primroses will bloom – all of that good stuff.

But other things will become impossible. You wont be able to build an igloo or a snow cave, or make ice candles, or drink eggnog (why would you?), or go to a panto, or hear Handel's Messiah (they don't perform it in summer), or send a Valentine, or attend midnight mass, or go to a Christmas market, or stay in an ice hotel, or make a snow-slide.

Neither will you be able to savour the opening of an Advent calendar, one window at a time, possibly the most beautifully long-drawn-out act of spiritual meditation in existence.

Don't spend the winter longing for warmer weather. That would be a waste of a season. We only get four!

Wishing for one of them to pass is perilous. Once you get into that mindset, you will spend spring waiting for the heat of summer, summer waiting for the coolness of autumn, and autumn waiting... for a snowball fight.